C. S. Lewis (1898-
Fully Lived

From a Reluctant Mind to a Transformed Life

Living Epistles – 40 Day Devotional Series|Book 2

By
C.S. Lewis; Zacharias Godseagle;
Amb. M. O. Ogbe;
C. Ladi Ogbe;

Table of Contents

COPYRIGHT © PAGE

C. S. Lewis (1898–1963) -Mere Christianity, Fully Lived From a Reluctant Mind to a Transformed Life

Living Epistles – 40 Day Devotional Series | Book 2

© Copyright © 2026

Zacharias Godseagle and

Godseagle Ministries

All rights reserved.

AUTHORS

C.S. Lewis

Zacharias Godseagle

Ambassador Monday O. Ogbe

Comfort Ladi Ogbe

PUBLISHER

Zacharias Godseagle and Godseagle Ministries

Published by: **Zacharias Godseagle**

Contact - **https://www.otakada.org**

ambassador@otakada.org

Tel/SMS +13024922440;

Whatsapp +2348032835348

DISCLAIMER

This book is a devotional and discipleship resource. While it draws from historical writings, including *The Confessions of St. Augustine*, it is not intended as a critical academic edition or a replacement for primary theological texts.

Scripture quotations are used for devotional and instructional purposes. Interpretations and applications are presented prayerfully and pastorally.

SCRIPTURE NOTICE

Unless otherwise indicated, Scripture quotations are taken from commonly used English translations. Emphasis has been added in places for clarity and devotional focus.

PRINTING INFORMATION

Printed in the United States of America
First Edition

ABOUT THE BOOK – C. S. Lewis (1898–1963) - Mere Christianity, Fully Lived

From a Reluctant Mind to a Transformed Life

What happens when Christianity is not merely believed—but *lived*?

BEFORE MERE CHRISTIANITY became one of the most influential Christian books of the twentieth century, its author was a reluctant convert—brilliant, wounded, skeptical, and resistant to God. C. S. Lewis did not arrive at faith easily, nor did he accept it sentimentally. He argued his way toward belief, resisted it fiercely, and finally surrendered to what he once called "the most dejected and reluctant conversion in all England."

This book begins there.

Mere Christianity, Fully Lived invites readers into a 40-day journey that brings Lewis's *ideas down into daily obedience*. Drawing from his early life, intellectual struggles, personal losses, wartime broadcasts, and enduring writings, this devotional does not merely explain Christianity—it **trains the reader to practice it**.

Many readers admire *Mere Christianity* yet struggle to apply it. Some find it profound but abstract. Others praise its clarity while wishing it spoke more directly to the pressures of modern life. This devotional responds to those long-standing tensions by doing what Lewis himself believed faith must do: **move from reason to action, from conviction to character**.

Each day combines:

- A **biographical moment** from Lewis's life
- A **core insight** drawn from *Mere Christianity* and related writings
- A **modern reflection** that translates Lewis's thought into everyday language
- A **practical action or spiritual exercise** that engages mind, heart, and will

Rather than overwhelming the reader with theology, this book unfolds formation gradually—allowing truth to take root through reflection, discipline, and lived response. Readers are not asked merely to agree with Lewis, but to **walk with him**, wrestling honestly with doubt, pride, suffering, obedience, and joy.

This is not a summary of *Mere Christianity*.

It is a **guided immersion**.

Not a biography alone.

Not an apologetics manual.

But a living epistle—written not on paper, but in the life of the reader.

If Augustine taught us the restless heart, Lewis teaches us the disciplined will.

And this book invites you to live what you believe—one day at a time.

WHO THIS BOOK IS FOR

This book is for readers who think deeply—and want to live faithfully.

It is written for those who admire *Mere Christianity* but sense that belief alone is not the end of the journey. For those who resonate with C. S. Lewis's clarity of thought, yet feel the daily tension between conviction and practice.

This book is for:

◈ Christians who believe the faith must engage both **mind and obedience**

◈ Readers shaped by doubt, reason, suffering, or intellectual honesty

◈ Seekers who want more than sentiment, but less than abstraction

◈ Believers longing for formation, not just information

◈ Readers navigating modern life who need ancient truth translated into lived reality

It is especially for those who have ever said:

- *"I believe this—but how do I live it?"*
- *"My faith makes sense, but my life hasn't caught up yet."*
- *"I want Christianity that forms character, not just opinion."*

This is not a book for passive reading.

It is for those willing to be shaped.

WHAT YOU WILL RECEIVE FROM THIS JOURNEY

This 40-day devotional journey is designed to **form the whole person**—mind, heart, and will.

Through daily readings, you will receive:

• **A Living Portrait of C. S. Lewis**

You will encounter Lewis not as a distant intellectual icon, but as a man shaped by grief, doubt, imagination, discipline, and reluctant surrender. His early life, struggles, and transformation provide a human framework for faith that feels honest and accessible.

- **Mere Christianity Translated into Daily Life**

Core ideas from *Mere Christianity* are re-expressed in contemporary language and applied to everyday realities—work, relationships, conscience, suffering, obedience, and joy.

- **Structured Spiritual Formation**

Each day follows a deliberate rhythm: reflection, insight, and response—allowing truth to move from understanding into practice.

- **Action-Driven Faith**

This journey does not ask you merely to agree with Christian truth. It invites you to practice it—through intentional exercises that shape habits, decisions, and character.

- **Gradual Depth, Not Overwhelm**

Rather than revealing everything at once, this devotional unfolds formation progressively, allowing space for reflection, resistance, and growth.

By the end of these forty days, readers will not simply know Lewis better.

They will understand themselves more honestly—and be better equipped to live what they believe.

SEVEN POWERFUL REVIEW QUOTES

"**Mere Christianity explains what Christians believe. This book helps you live it.**"

"**Lewis doesn't water down the faith—and this devotional doesn't either. It challenges the reader to obedience, not just agreement.**"

"**Few books have shaped modern Christianity like *Mere Christianity*. This devotional finally brings its ideas into daily practice.**"

"**C. S. Lewis speaks to the modern mind because he first wrestled with doubt himself. This book captures that honesty beautifully.**"

"**Clear, bracing, and deeply practical—Lewis's thought comes alive when paired with daily action.**"

"**This is not sentimental devotion. It is thoughtful, demanding, and deeply rewarding.**"

"**Lewis meets the reader where they are—but never lets them stay there.**"

Shalom!

Zacharias Godseagle; Amb M. O. Ogbe; C. Ladi Ogbe
God's Eagle Ministries
https://www.otakada.org
ambassador@otakada.org

PAPERBACK BACK-COVER BLURB

Mere Christianity explained the faith. - This book helps you live it.

Before C. S. Lewis became one of Christianity's most influential voices, he was a reluctant convert—brilliant, wounded, skeptical, and resistant to God. His journey from doubt to surrender shaped *Mere Christianity*, a book that has guided millions toward faith.

Mere Christianity, Fully Lived invites readers to go further.

This 40-day devotional blends Lewis's early life, core insights from *Mere Christianity*, and practical daily application into a journey of lived formation. Rather than summarizing theology, it trains the reader to practice it—day by day.

Each reflection combines biography, timeless Christian truth, modern language, and intentional action, helping belief move from the page into everyday life.

This is not merely a devotional.

It is an invitation to formation.

Not simply to think like a Christian—

but to live like one.

Living Epistles – where faith becomes visible.

DEDICATION

To all who believe—
  and to those who struggle to believe;
to minds that seek clarity,
hearts that long for honesty,
and lives still being written by the grace of God.
For readers on the long road
from reason to surrender,
from faith examined
to faith fully lived.

ACKNOWLEDGEMENTS

This work stands on the shoulders of faith thoughtfully examined and courageously lived.

We are deeply grateful for the enduring witness of **C. S. Lewis**, whose intellectual honesty, imaginative clarity, and humble obedience continue to guide countless readers toward a deeper and more durable Christianity. Though separated by time, his voice remains strikingly present—calling modern minds to reckon with truth, goodness, and the person of Christ not as an abstract idea, but as a living Lord.

We acknowledge the many scholars, teachers, pastors, and writers whose careful preservation and interpretation of Lewis's life and writings have made this devotional journey possible. Their labor has helped ensure that faith informed by reason remains accessible to each new generation.

We are also thankful for the global community of readers—seekers, skeptics, believers, and strugglers—whose questions, reflections, and honest critiques have shaped the vision of this book. Many of the themes addressed here arise from real tensions voiced by readers of *Mere Christianity*: the desire for clarity without coldness, conviction without pride, and belief that transforms daily life rather than remaining theoretical.

Special thanks are due to those who contributed to the devotional framing and spiritual application of this work. Your prayerful discernment helped shape this book not merely as a reflection on Lewis's ideas, but as an invitation to live them.

Above all, we acknowledge God—who meets reluctant minds with patience, pursues wandering hearts with grace, and continues to write living epistles through ordinary lives surrendered to His will.

May this work serve not as an endpoint, but as a beginning.

PUBLISHER ACKNOWLEDGEMENT

This volume is published as part of the **Living Epistles – 40 Day Devotional Series**, a discipleship initiative devoted to forming believers whose faith is not only confessed, but embodied.

The series began with *St. Augustine of Hippo (354–430 AD): From a Restless Heart to a Written Life*, which traced Augustine's journey from inward turmoil to surrendered obedience. That first volume established the central conviction of this work: that God continues to write His truth through yielded lives, and that the testimonies of faithful men and women remain living instruction for the Church today.

The first volume in the Living Epistles series is available here: **https://www.amazon.com/ST-AUGUSTINE-HIPPO-354-430-Devotional-ebook/dp/B0GJN8N9XS**

Mere Christianity, Fully Lived continues this vision by turning to the life and thought of **C. S. Lewis**, whose reluctant conversion and disciplined faith speak powerfully to the modern mind. Where Augustine revealed the restless heart, Lewis confronts the resistant will—calling believers beyond belief into daily obedience.

Godseagle Ministries publishes the Living Epistles series with a clear mandate: to steward Scripture-centered resources that disciple nations, strengthen the Church, and equip believers to live visibly as ambassadors of Christ. We believe that faith is not sustained by ideas alone, but by lives shaped through truth, tested by obedience, and empowered by the Spirit of God.

Each volume in this series is offered prayerfully, with the hope that readers will not merely learn from the past, but respond in the present—allowing God to continue writing His living epistles through ordinary lives surrendered to His purposes.

We are grateful for every reader who enters this journey, trusting that the same God who transformed Augustine and Lewis is still at work today.

PREFACE

C hristianity has never been sustained by ideas alone.
It has always been carried forward through lives.

From Abraham's obedience to Paul's surrender, from Augustine's restless confession to the reluctant yielding of **C. S. Lewis**, God has chosen to make Himself known not only through written revelation, but through embodied faith. Scripture reveals truth; lives demonstrate what that truth looks like when it is believed, resisted, tested, and finally obeyed.

This book was written with that conviction.

Mere Christianity has helped millions understand what Christians believe. It has clarified doctrine, dismantled confusion, and spoken persuasively to thoughtful minds across generations. Yet many readers have sensed a quiet gap between understanding and living—between agreement and obedience. This devotional was born to meet that gap.

C. S. Lewis himself understood it well. His journey toward Christ was not marked by emotional enthusiasm or instant certainty, but by long resistance, careful reasoning, and an eventual surrender that cost him control. He believed before he obeyed. He argued before he knelt. And when he finally yielded, he did so not because faith felt easy, but because truth left him no alternative.

That tension—between conviction and transformation—remains deeply modern.

We live in an age rich with information and poor in formation. Many believers know what they believe, yet struggle to live it consistently. Faith is affirmed, but compartmentalized. Christ is admired, but not always followed. Lewis saw this danger clearly and insisted that Christianity, if true, must remake us—not merely inspire us.

This book invites you into that same reckoning.

Mere Christianity, Fully Lived is not a study guide, nor a biography in the conventional sense. It is a 40-day journey designed to help belief take on flesh through daily reflection, honest self-examination, and intentional response. Drawing from Lewis's early life, his reluctant conversion, and the enduring insights of *Mere Christianity*, each day invites you to move beyond passive agreement into practiced obedience.

The days ahead are arranged deliberately. They do not rush, nor do they overwhelm. Truth is allowed to unfold gradually, giving space for resistance, recognition, and response. Some days will clarify. Others may unsettle. A few may confront habits or assumptions long left unexamined. That is intentional. Formation rarely happens without friction.

This book does not ask you to become like C. S. Lewis.

It invites you to become what Lewis himself believed every Christian is called to be: a life in which Christ is not merely acknowledged, but expressed.

As you begin, come honestly.

You do not need certainty—only willingness.

You do not need perfection—only surrender.

The goal of this journey is not to finish forty readings, but to begin a different way of living. May these pages serve not as an endpoint, but as a doorway—into faith that is thoughtful, disciplined, and fully lived.

EARLY READER REVIEW

"I've read *Mere Christianity* more than once, but this devotional finally helped me slow down and let its truths change my daily habits."

"This book doesn't let you hide behind admiration for Lewis. It gently but firmly asks what obedience actually looks like."

"The blend of biography, reflection, and action made this feel like a guided spiritual apprenticeship rather than a devotional."

"What surprised me most was how personal this became. Lewis's early struggles mirrored my own far more than I expected."

"Thoughtful without being heavy, challenging without being harsh. This is a devotional for people who want their faith to mature."

"I appreciated that this wasn't rushed. Each day built on the last, giving space for conviction, resistance, and growth."

"By the end of the forty days, I realized this wasn't just about Lewis or *Mere Christianity*. It was about how I was actually living."

INTRODUCTION

"You are our epistle, written in our hearts, known and read by all people."
— 2 Corinthians 3:2

Christianity was never meant to remain theoretical.

It was not given merely to be defended, explained, or admired, but to be **embodied**—to take visible shape in ordinary lives surrendered to an extraordinary Christ. The gospel does not end with belief; it begins there. Its true witness is not found only in books, but in people whose lives have been reoriented by truth.

This is the conviction behind the **Living Epistles** series.

Each volume is built on a simple but demanding idea: that the lives of those who wrestled honestly with God, truth, and obedience still speak—not as distant history, but as living instruction. Their struggles, failures, delays, and eventual surrender reveal how faith takes root in real human experience.

In this volume, we turn to **C. S. Lewis (1898–1963)**—not because he lived a flawless Christian life, but because he lived a *truthful* one.

Lewis did not begin as a believer eager for obedience. He began as a reluctant mind—sharp, imaginative, wounded, and resistant to God. He loved reason, beauty, and moral clarity, yet resisted the authority that Christianity demanded. His journey toward Christ was not swift or sentimental; it was marked by argument, delay, and surrender that came at a cost.

That makes his voice especially relevant now.

We live in an age where belief is easy to profess, but obedience is often postponed. Faith is discussed, debated, and shared, yet rarely allowed to reorder life completely. Many people agree with Christianity in principle while negotiating its demands in practice. Lewis recognized this tension clearly and insisted that Christianity, if true, leaves no room for comfortable neutrality.

This book invites you into that same reckoning.

Mere Christianity, Fully Lived is not an introduction to Lewis's thought, nor a replacement for his writings. It is a **guided journey** that brings his life, his ideas, and the claims of Christ into conversation with your own daily experience. It does not rush to answers, but it does not allow avoidance. It asks what Lewis himself had to face: *If this is true, then how must I live?*

The chapters that follow are designed to move slowly and deliberately. You will encounter moments from Lewis's early life, insights drawn from *Mere Christianity*, and reflections that translate those truths into modern language. Each step prepares the ground for what comes next, allowing space for recognition before response, and conviction before action.

You are not expected to arrive with certainty.

You are invited to arrive with honesty.

The goal of this journey is not to admire C. S. Lewis, nor even to master Christian ideas, but to examine how belief becomes obedience—how truth becomes visible in habits, decisions, relationships, and character.

Before the day-by-day journey begins, the next section will help you linger where Lewis himself lingered: in the space between resistance and surrender, between knowing and yielding. There, the groundwork is laid for faith that does not remain theoretical, but becomes fully lived.

INTRODUCTION TO PART ONE
BEFORE MERE CHRISTIANITY

The Making of a Reluctant Soul

Before Christianity became something to be explained, defended, or lived, it was something **resisted**.

Part One of this book does not begin with belief.

It begins with formation.

Long before *Mere Christianity* was written, the life that would produce it was being quietly shaped—by loss, longing, imagination, intellect, and an unyielded will. These early forces did not lead C. S. Lewis directly to faith. They prepared him for a reckoning he could not avoid.

This section invites you to linger there.

Here, Lewis is not yet the Christian thinker so many admire. He is a boy wounded by grief, a young man awakened by beauty, a disciplined mind resistant to authority, and an honest skeptic unwilling to surrender without reason. His questions are not shallow, his resistance not careless. He believes truth matters—and that belief itself becomes costly.

This is why his story remains so recognizably modern.

Many people today do not reject Christianity outright. They postpone it. They admire it. They keep it at a distance while remaining deeply formed by experiences that make surrender feel unsafe. Faith is not dismissed; it is delayed. Obedience is not denied; it is negotiated.

Part One traces how this posture takes shape.

These chapters are not meant to convince you.

They are meant to **help you recognize yourself**.

You are not asked to agree or disagree yet.

You are asked to notice—how loss teaches caution, how longing awakens desire, how reason demands honesty, how conscience refuses silence, and how surrender often feels like defeat before it becomes freedom.

This is the soil from which *Mere Christianity* grew.

It is also the soil many readers still stand upon.

Before belief becomes obedience, formation has already begun.

What follows is not a defense of belief, nor a roadmap to faith.

It is a tracing of formation.

Before Christianity became something C. S. Lewis would explain to others, it was something he resisted within himself. His questions did not arise in a vacuum; they were shaped by loss, longing, imagination, and a disciplined refusal to surrender without honesty.

Part One enters that interior world.

These chapters do not rush toward conclusions. They move slowly, deliberately, through the forces that shaped a reluctant soul—forces that still shape many lives today. Here, belief has not yet become obedience. Faith has not yet become personal. But the ground is being prepared.

The journey begins where resistance still feels reasonable.

CHAPTER ONE
BEFORE BELIEF BECAME OBEDIENCE

How a Reluctant Soul Was Prepared for Truth

Long before **C. S. Lewis** became one of the most trusted voices in Christian thought, he was a boy shaped by grief, imagination, and an unrelenting hunger for meaning.

Lewis's story does not begin with faith.

It begins with **loss**.

At a young age, Lewis lost his mother. The wound was not merely emotional—it rearranged his inner world. Safety vanished. Certainty cracked. God, if He existed at all, seemed distant or unreliable. Like many today who encounter pain early, Lewis learned to survive by turning inward—into books, imagination, and later, intellect. He built a world where meaning could be controlled, where reason replaced trust, and where longing could be named without being answered.

This, too, feels modern.

Many people today did not reject Christianity because they examined it carefully. They drifted from it because life hurt early, questions went unanswered, or authority failed them. Faith did not collapse under argument—it quietly eroded under disappointment.

Lewis's early life trained him to think fiercely, but to trust cautiously.

As he grew, his imagination flourished. Myth, legend, poetry, and story awakened in him a deep sense that reality must mean more than survival and pleasure. He sensed that beauty pointed beyond itself, that longing hinted at something real. Yet when Christianity presented itself, he resisted it with vigor. He did not deny morality. He did not deny beauty. He denied **submission**. God, if real, would demand more than Lewis was ready to give.

So he delayed.

Many modern readers recognize this posture instantly.

They believe there is "something more," yet hesitate to name it God.

They admire Christ, yet hesitate to follow Him.

They long for meaning, yet fear surrender.

Lewis lived for years in this space—what might be called **honest resistance**. He did not pretend disbelief was effortless. He admitted that the moral law pressed on him. He knew right and wrong felt real, binding, unavoidable. And yet he also knew that if Christianity were true, it would require not adjustment, but **yielding**.

This tension—between knowing and obeying—eventually shaped the heart of **Mere Christianity**.

Mere Christianity was not written as a triumphant declaration of belief. It was forged in the slow fire of intellectual surrender. Lewis had argued himself into a corner where honesty demanded a decision. He famously described himself as "the most reluctant convert in all England." His conversion was not marked by emotional ecstasy, but by a quiet collapse of resistance.

That, too, speaks to our time.

In a world saturated with information, belief often comes easily. Obedience does not. We accumulate sermons, podcasts, books, and quotes, yet remain curiously unchanged. We negotiate with Christ instead of kneeling before Him. Lewis recognized this as the central modern problem—not ignorance, but **half-surrender**.

Mere Christianity emerged as Lewis tried to explain what he himself was learning: that Christianity is not about becoming nicer people, but about becoming new ones. Not about managing behavior, but about undergoing transformation. Not about adding God to our lives, but about allowing God to reorder everything.

His earlier life—marked by grief, imagination, intellectual pride, and reluctant yielding—gave him a unique voice. He could speak to skeptics without contempt and to believers without flattery. He understood the modern soul because he had lived inside it.

And so when Lewis writes about pride, he is not theorizing.

When he writes about morality, he is not abstracting.

When he writes about Christ, he is describing Someone who disrupted his carefully ordered inner world.

The enduring power of *Mere Christianity* lies here: it does not allow readers to remain observers. It quietly insists that if Christianity is true, then neutrality is impossible. Christ must be either resisted or obeyed.

This is why Lewis's work continues to cut across generations, cultures, and denominations. He does not appeal only to religious insiders. He speaks to the hesitant, the thoughtful, the wounded, and the quietly restless. He writes for those who sense that belief without transformation is hollow—and that transformation without surrender is impossible.

This journey begins where Lewis himself once stood:

between admiration and obedience,

between understanding and yielding,

between a self-directed life and a Christ-directed one.

You are not being asked to agree with Lewis.

You are being invited to examine the same interior questions that shaped him—and to notice where those questions already live within you.

The chapters that follow will not rush you.

They will not overwhelm you.

But they will not leave you untouched.

For now, it is enough to recognize this:

long before faith becomes action, it must become **personal**.

The journey does not begin with answers.

It begins with honesty.

INFLECTION POINTS

Questions for Honest Self-Examination

THESE QUESTIONS ARE not meant to be answered quickly.
They are meant to be noticed.
Allow them to surface recognition rather than resolution.

1. **Where in your own story did belief become complicated—not by argument, but by experience?**
   What moments quietly reshaped how safe faith felt to you?
2. **In what ways do you find it easier to think about faith than to yield to it?**
   Where has understanding replaced surrender?
3. **What truths do you agree with that you have not yet obeyed?**
   Be specific, not general.
4. **How do you personally delay obedience?**
   Through analysis? Distraction? Good intentions postponed?
5. **What would obedience cost you right now—not hypothetically, but concretely?**
   What control, identity, or security feels threatened?
6. **Have you ever sensed that Christianity was true, yet resisted it because of what it might demand?**
   Sit honestly with that tension.
7. **Where might admiration for Christ be functioning as a substitute for following Him?**
   What feels respectable—but unyielded?
8. **If neutrality were not an option, what would need to change in your life?**
   Do not answer—only notice what surfaces.

Gentle Orientation for the Reader
You are not asked to move yet.
You are asked to *see*.

Before belief becomes obedience,
truth must become personal.

CHAPTER TWO
Loss, Longing, and the Birth of Resistance

When Pain Shapes the Way We Believe

L ong before belief becomes a matter of doctrine, it is shaped by experience. For **C. S. Lewis**, loss did more than cause grief—it quietly trained his instincts. The death of his mother did not simply leave an absence; it introduced a question that would linger for years: *Can anything truly be trusted to last?*

Pain has a way of doing that. It does not always harden the heart outright. More often, it teaches the heart to protect itself.

Lewis did not respond to loss by rejecting meaning. Instead, he searched for it relentlessly—but on his own terms. He learned early how fragile affection could be, how unreliable comfort seemed, how quickly security could dissolve. And so he began to build inner defenses—not walls of bitterness, but structures of control.

This, too, feels unmistakably modern.

Many people today carry wounds they rarely name. Childhood disappointments. Unmet expectations. Authority figures who failed them. Prayers that felt unanswered. Rather than confronting these losses directly, they learn to compensate—to rely on competence, independence, intellect, or self-sufficiency. Faith is not rejected outright; it is kept at a careful distance.

Lewis's resistance to God was not rooted in indifference. It was shaped by caution.

He longed deeply—for beauty, for joy, for something beyond the visible world. Yet he feared that to trust fully would be to risk disappointment again. God, if real, would not merely offer comfort; He would demand surrender. And surrender felt unsafe.

So Lewis learned to admire from afar.

This pattern is familiar to many. We allow longing to exist, but we regulate its reach. We acknowledge desire, but we refuse vulnerability. We say we are open to truth—as long as it does not require us to release control.

Loss trains us to calculate.

Lewis's imagination gave him glimpses of something more—moments of piercing joy, fleeting experiences of beauty that hinted at a reality beyond the material world. But these experiences did not immediately lead him to God. Instead, they deepened the tension. If such longing pointed to something real, then reality itself might demand response.

And response meant risk.

So Lewis learned to analyze longing instead of obeying it. He named it. Studied it. Contained it. This allowed him to remain intellectually honest without becoming personally exposed. He could explore meaning without kneeling before it.

Again, this feels deeply contemporary.

We live in a culture that encourages exploration without commitment. We analyze faith, discuss spirituality, and consume insight—yet resist anything that would reorder our lives. Longing is treated as an experience to manage, not a signal to follow.

Lewis's resistance was shaped here, in this careful posture: open enough to question, closed enough to remain in control.

But longing has a way of refusing containment.

The very desires Lewis tried to manage became persistent reminders that something—or Someone—stood beyond his defenses. Loss had trained him to distrust permanence, yet longing insisted that permanence existed. Pain had taught him to guard himself, yet joy suggested that surrender might be worth the risk.

This inner conflict would become one of the defining tensions of his life.

Lewis would later write about desire not as something to be satisfied by earthly substitutes, but as a signpost pointing beyond them. Yet before he could articulate this insight, he had to confront its implications personally. Longing could not be neutral. It demanded interpretation—and eventually, response.

For many modern readers, this chapter touches a sensitive place.

We may not identify as skeptics. We may even identify as believers. Yet we recognize the instinct to manage faith carefully—to allow belief without exposure, agreement without vulnerability, admiration without obedience. Loss teaches us caution. Longing teaches us restlessness. Between the two, resistance quietly takes root.

Lewis's story reminds us that resistance is not always rebellion. Sometimes it is self-protection disguised as wisdom.

But Christianity does not remain content with guarded admiration. If true, it presses gently but persistently against our defenses. It asks whether our caution has become avoidance—and whether our longing is calling us beyond control.

This chapter does not ask you to resolve that tension yet.

It only asks you to notice it.

Longing is not accidental.

Loss is not meaningless.

Both shape the way we approach God.

Before belief becomes obedience, these forces must be named.

Only then can the journey continue honestly.

INFLECTION POINTS

Questions for Honest Noticing

DO NOT RUSH THESE QUESTIONS.
They are not meant to be answered fully yet.
Some are meant only to be recognized.

1. **What early loss or disappointment shaped the way you learned to trust—or not trust—God?**
Consider not only dramatic losses, but quiet ones: unmet expectations, unanswered prayers, broken authority.

2. **In what ways have you learned to protect yourself from disappointment by staying in control?**
Where has caution slowly replaced openness?

3. **What do you allow yourself to admire from a distance, but resist fully engaging?**
Is there a version of faith you find beautiful—but unsafe?

4. **How do you typically respond to longing—for meaning, depth, or permanence?**
Do you pursue it, analyze it, distract yourself from it, or contain it?

5. **Where might self-protection be disguising itself as wisdom or maturity?**
What feels "reasonable" that may actually be avoidance?

6. **If longing is not accidental, what might it be pointing toward in your life right now?**
What would it mean to take that signal seriously?

7. **What feels most risky about surrender—not in theory, but in practice?**
What do you fear you might lose?

8. **Have you ever delayed obedience not because you disagreed with truth, but because yielding felt unsafe?**
Sit with that distinction.

Gentle Orientation for the Reader

You are not asked to resolve these questions yet.
Only to let them surface honestly.
Longing and resistance often grow together.
Naming them is the first act of truth.

CHAPTER THREE
Imagination Without Surrender

When Beauty Awakens Desire but Stops Short of Obedience

For **C. S. Lewis**, imagination was not an escape from reality—it was an awakening to it.

Long before he believed in God, Lewis believed in meaning. Beauty moved him. Story stirred him. Myth opened windows his intellect alone could not. Through poetry, legend, and ancient tales, he sensed that reality carried weight beyond survival and pleasure. There was something *more*—something persistent, luminous, and just out of reach.

Imagination taught Lewis to long.

Yet imagination, by itself, did not teach him how to yield.

Lewis's early experiences of beauty produced moments of intense desire—what he later called *joy*. These moments were not satisfied by the objects that triggered them. A line of poetry, a story, a memory of nature—each awakened longing, then faded, leaving behind an ache. The experience was unmistakable, but its meaning remained unresolved.

He learned something crucial early on: desire could be awakened without being fulfilled.

This discovery shaped him deeply.

Rather than leading him immediately toward God, imagination became a space where Lewis could experience transcendence without commitment. He could explore wonder without surrender, beauty without obedience, longing without allegiance. Imagination allowed him to remain open without being vulnerable.

This posture is not uncommon.

Many people today are deeply moved by beauty—music, art, story, justice, even spirituality—yet resist naming its source. They experience longing but avoid its implications. They allow imagination to stir the soul while keeping the will firmly in control.

Imagination becomes a safe middle ground.

Lewis's intellect analyzed these experiences carefully. He studied desire instead of following it. He examined longing instead of submitting to what it suggested. This allowed him to remain honest about his experiences while postponing their demands.

But imagination, once awakened, refuses to remain neutral.

The very beauty Lewis encountered began to trouble him. If longing was not random—if it pointed beyond the material world—then reality itself might be structured toward something greater. And if that were true, imagination was not merely decorative. It was diagnostic.

It was pointing.

Lewis began to sense that his deepest desires were not meant to be satisfied by the things that awakened them. They were signposts, not destinations. Yet to follow those signposts would require more than imagination. It would require surrender.

And surrender still felt costly.

So Lewis lingered in admiration. He allowed beauty to instruct his emotions while resisting its authority over his life. He appreciated the pull of transcendence without bowing to it. Imagination gave him language for longing, but not courage for obedience.

This tension—between seeing and yielding—runs quietly through modern faith as well.

Many people today are moved by Christianity's beauty but hesitate before its demands. They admire Christ's teaching, resonate with the story of redemption, and feel drawn to the vision of transformed life—yet resist the claim that this beauty requires reorientation of the self.

Imagination awakens desire.

Obedience requires decision.

Lewis's journey reminds us that imagination is a gift, but it is not an endpoint. It can prepare the heart, but it cannot complete the work. Beauty can call us toward truth, but it cannot compel us to kneel.

Eventually, Lewis would come to see that imagination was not misleading him—but it was not sufficient on its own. Longing was not meant to be managed indefinitely. It was meant to lead somewhere.

This chapter does not resolve that tension.

It simply names it.

Before belief becomes obedience, imagination often awakens the soul.

But surrender must still follow.

INFLECTION POINTS

Questions for Honest Noticing

DO NOT RUSH THESE QUESTIONS.

Let them surface recognition, not answers.

1. **What experiences of beauty, story, or meaning have awakened longing in you?**
   When have you felt that quiet sense that life points beyond itself?
2. **How do you usually respond to that longing?**
   Do you pursue it, analyze it, contain it, or distract yourself from it?
3. **Where have you allowed imagination to stir your faith without allowing it to shape your obedience?**
   What feels inspiring—but safely distant?
4. **Are there aspects of Christianity you find beautiful but resist submitting to?**
   Name them honestly.
5. **In what ways might admiration be functioning as a substitute for allegiance?**
   Where does appreciation stop short of commitment?
6. **If longing is a signpost rather than a destination, where might it be pointing you right now?**
   Do not answer—only notice.
7. **What feels most threatening about allowing beauty to lead to obedience?**
   What control might be at stake?

Gentle Orientation for the Reader
Imagination is not the enemy of faith.
But neither is it the finish line.
Longing prepares the heart.
Surrender prepares the life.

CHAPTER FOUR
The Honest Atheist

When Doubt Refuses to Be Shallow

Before **C. S. Lewis** surrendered to faith, he became something far rarer than a casual skeptic—he became an *honest* one.

Lewis did not reject Christianity out of convenience, rebellion, or indifference. His unbelief was not flippant. It was principled, reasoned, and disciplined. He believed that if truth mattered, then false comfort was a greater danger than discomfort. And so he refused belief until he was convinced it could withstand scrutiny.

This distinction matters.

Much modern doubt is thin. It avoids commitment without engaging consequences. Lewis's doubt was thick. It wrestled. It stayed awake at night. It followed arguments to their uncomfortable conclusions. He did not want Christianity to be true if it required intellectual dishonesty. And if it *was* true, he knew he could not afford to treat it lightly.

Lewis's atheism was shaped not by hostility toward goodness, but by loyalty to reason.

He believed the universe was ultimately indifferent—beautiful, perhaps, but impersonal. Meaning was something humans projected, not something they received. Morality was useful, but not binding. Desire was real, but its object was imagined. This worldview allowed Lewis to remain intellectually coherent while avoiding the authority that Christianity implied.

Yet coherence has limits.

Lewis began to notice cracks in his unbelief—not emotional cracks, but logical ones. If the universe was truly indifferent, why did moral obligation feel unavoidable? Why did right and wrong press upon the conscience with such authority? Why did injustice provoke outrage rather than mere dislike?

He found himself defending moral judgments that his worldview could not fully support.

This disturbed him.

Lewis realized that he was borrowing moral certainty from a universe his atheism could not explain. He lived as though some things were truly wrong—not merely inconvenient or socially disapproved, but *objectively wrong*. This recognition did not push him toward faith immediately, but it unsettled his confidence in unbelief.

Honest doubt has a way of doing that.

Rather than resolving this tension quickly, Lewis stayed with it. He allowed doubt to examine itself. He resisted the temptation to soften questions or retreat into sentiment. He followed reason where it led—even when it pointed beyond the boundaries he preferred.

This is why Lewis remains so compelling to modern readers.

He does not dismiss doubt.

He does not mock skepticism.

He honors honest questioning while exposing its limits.

Many people today resonate deeply with this posture. They want faith that respects reason. They refuse belief that demands intellectual shortcuts. Yet they also sense that doubt, left unchecked, can become a refuge—a place where responsibility is postponed and obedience deferred.

Lewis's story exposes this possibility gently but firmly.

There is a difference between doubt that seeks truth and doubt that seeks delay. One is courageous. The other is protective. Lewis discovered that his unbelief, though honest, was also costly. It allowed him to avoid surrender, but it could not finally explain the world he inhabited.

Eventually, he would recognize that Christianity did not violate reason—it completed it. But that recognition lay ahead.

For now, Lewis stood in a difficult but honorable place: unwilling to believe dishonestly, yet increasingly unable to disbelieve comfortably.

This chapter does not argue you into faith.

It asks something more subtle.

It asks whether your doubts are doing the work you believe they are doing—or whether they have quietly become a shelter from decision.

INFLECTION POINTS

Questions for Honest Noticing

DO NOT RUSH TO DEFEND yourself as you read these.
Let them surface quietly.

1. **How would you describe your own doubts—are they curious, cautious, defensive, or unresolved?**
   What tone do they carry?
2. **Have you ever delayed obedience while telling yourself you were still "thinking things through"?**
   What might that delay be protecting?
3. **Where do you expect Christianity to meet your standards before you consider yielding to it?**
   Are those standards reasonable—or controlling?
4. **Do your doubts push you toward truth, or do they allow you to remain undecided indefinitely?**
   Sit honestly with that distinction.
5. **What moral convictions do you hold that feel unavoidable or binding?**
   Where do you believe those convictions come from?
6. **Have you ever noticed tension between what you say you believe about reality and how you live within it?**
   What does that tension reveal?
7. **If Christianity were true, what would your doubt be protecting you from right now?**
   Do not answer—only notice.

GENTLE ORIENTATION for the Reader

Honest doubt is not the enemy of faith.
But neither is it a permanent home.
At some point, truth asks to be obeyed—not merely examined.

CHAPTER FIVE
The Moral Law We Cannot Silence

Why Right and Wrong Refuse to Be Negotiated

As **C. S. Lewis** examined his unbelief more carefully, one reality refused to stay quiet: the stubborn presence of *ought*.

He noticed that human beings did not merely prefer certain behaviors—they *expected* them. We argued as though fairness mattered. We excused ourselves as though we knew we had fallen short. We condemned cruelty not as inconvenient, but as wrong. And we did this instinctively, across cultures and circumstances, even when it cost us nothing to remain silent.

This disturbed Lewis.

If the universe were truly indifferent, moral obligation should feel optional. Yet it did not. Right and wrong pressed upon the conscience with a weight that could not be explained away as mere instinct or social conditioning. People disagreed about moral details, but they rarely emphasized disagreement itself. Instead, they argued as though a shared standard existed—and as though others ought to recognize it.

Lewis recognized this tension everywhere.

We excuse our behavior by appealing to fairness.

We defend ourselves by explaining intention.

We accuse others as though justice were real.

Even when we violate our own standards, we do not deny their existence. We appeal to them.

This observation would later become foundational to **Mere Christianity**, but long before Lewis wrote about it, he wrestled with its implications personally.

Where did this moral law come from?

If it was merely instinct, why did we feel justified in correcting it?

If it was merely culture, why did we judge cultures—including our own?

If it was merely preference, why did it bind us even when inconvenient?

Lewis began to see that moral obligation behaved less like a human invention and more like a discovery—something encountered rather than created. And if that were true, then reality itself might be moral in nature.

This was an uncomfortable thought.

A moral universe implies accountability.

Accountability implies authority.

Authority implies Someone beyond ourselves.

Lewis did not rush to this conclusion, but he could not ignore where reason was pointing. He realized that his atheism explained many things elegantly—but not conscience. It could describe behavior, but not obligation. It could analyze desire, but not responsibility.

The moral law did not flatter him.

It did not excuse him.

It accused him.

This is why Lewis understood that morality is not comforting. It does not simply tell us how to live well; it reveals how far we fall short. It exposes the gap between what we know we ought to do and what we actually do.

Modern readers recognize this tension immediately.

We speak passionately about justice, integrity, and compassion—yet excuse ourselves when those standards demand sacrifice. We are quick to identify wrongdoing in others, slower to acknowledge it in ourselves. We live as though moral truth exists, yet resist submitting to it fully.

The moral law reveals something unsettling: we are not merely mistaken. We are inconsistent.

Lewis saw that this inconsistency was not peripheral to faith—it was central. Christianity did not begin by telling people how good they were. It began by telling them the truth: that something had gone wrong, and that self-effort alone could not repair it.

The moral law, then, was not merely an ethical guide. It was a diagnosis.

It told Lewis that humanity was not simply ignorant, but estranged—not merely uninformed, but misaligned. And if that diagnosis was accurate, then improvement would not be enough. Transformation would be required.

This realization moved Lewis closer to Christianity—but not comfortably. The moral law did not simply point toward God; it pointed toward his own need. It challenged his independence. It unsettled his self-sufficiency. It demanded response, not admiration.

Yet Lewis lingered here, allowing the weight of this truth to press upon him.

Before belief becomes obedience, conscience must be taken seriously.

Not explained away.

Not managed.

Not silenced.

The moral law refuses to disappear because it is not ours to dismiss.

INFLECTION POINTS

Questions for Honest Noticing

DO NOT ANSWER THESE quickly.

Let them reveal patterns rather than conclusions.

1. **When you accuse others of wrongdoing, what standard are you appealing to?**
   Where do you believe that standard comes from?
2. **How do you usually explain your own moral failures?**
   By intention? Circumstance? Comparison?
3. **Are there moral convictions you expect others to honor but struggle to obey yourself?**
   Sit honestly with that tension.
4. **What does your conscience tend to accuse you of most often?**
   What does that reveal about what you value?
5. **Have you ever felt that you knew what was right—but resisted it anyway?**
   What did that resistance cost you?
6. **If moral obligation is real, what does it demand of you right now?**
   Do not act yet—only notice.
7. **What would change if right and wrong were not negotiable, but**

binding?
What would need to be reordered?

Gentle Orientation for the Reader
The moral law does not exist to shame us.
It exists to tell the truth.
Before grace can be received,
truth must be faced.

CHAPTER SIX
When Yielding Feels Like Defeat

Why Surrender Often Comes Last

By the time **C. S. Lewis** stood on the threshold of belief, the problem was no longer intellectual.

The arguments had narrowed.

The alternatives had thinned.

The moral law had pressed too firmly to be ignored.

What remained was not a question of truth, but of **will**.

Lewis discovered that the final resistance to Christianity was not disbelief—it was fear. To yield was to lose something. To submit was to relinquish control. Christianity, if true, did not simply ask to be considered. It asked to be obeyed.

And obedience felt like defeat.

This is the moment many never name.

We often imagine surrender as relief, but it rarely feels that way at first. It feels like loss—of autonomy, of authorship, of the right to define ourselves on our own terms. Lewis did not resist God because he loved darkness; he resisted because he loved independence.

He understood that belief alone would change little. Yielding would change everything.

To acknowledge God was one thing.

To submit to Him was another.

Lewis sensed that Christianity did not come merely to advise him, but to **take over**. It did not offer partnership; it demanded allegiance. And allegiance meant that Lewis would no longer be the final authority in his own life.

That realization slowed him.

Many modern readers recognize this hesitation immediately. We may assent to Christian truth, agree with Christian values, and even admire Christ—yet resist allowing Him authority over decisions, desires, time, or identity. Faith feels manageable as long as it remains advisory.

But Christianity does not remain advisory.

Lewis described his conversion not as a triumphant moment of joy, but as a reluctant capitulation. He felt himself being drawn, cornered, pursued—not against his will, but beyond his control. What finally gave way was not reason, but resistance.

Yielding felt like defeat because it required him to admit that he was not self-sufficient, not sovereign, not self-made.

And yet—this defeat would later reveal itself as freedom.

But not yet.

At this stage of his journey, Lewis lingered at the edge. He knew that once he crossed it, neutrality would be gone. He could no longer observe Christianity from a safe distance. He would have to live inside it.

This hesitation is deeply human.

We delay not because we do not know enough, but because we know enough to be afraid. Surrender exposes us. It confronts our carefully managed selves. It demands trust where we have learned to protect.

Lewis's resistance reminds us that surrender is not primarily emotional—it is existential. It redefines who holds authority over our lives. And authority, once yielded, cannot be reclaimed without consequence.

This chapter does not celebrate surrender yet.

It tells the truth about its cost.

Before belief becomes obedience, we must face what obedience will require.

Yielding often feels like defeat

because it ends the reign of the self.

INFLECTION POINTS

Questions for Honest Noticing

DO NOT ANSWER DEFENSIVELY.
Let these questions name what is real.

1. **What feels most costly about surrendering control of your life to God?**
   Be specific.
2. **Where do you prefer Christianity to advise rather than command?**
   What areas of life feel off-limits?
3. **Have you ever delayed obedience not because you doubted truth, but because yielding felt like loss?**
   What were you protecting?
4. **What authority do you currently resist yielding—over time, decisions, relationships, or identity?**
   Sit with that resistance.
5. **Do you associate surrender more with defeat than with freedom?**
   Why do you think that is?
6. **If neutrality were no longer an option, what would change first in your life?**
   Do not act—only notice.
7. **What version of yourself might have to die for obedience to begin?**
   Let that question remain open.

Gentle Orientation for the Reader
Surrender is rarely dramatic.
It is often quiet, reluctant, and costly.
But it is never meaningless.

INTRODUCTION TO PART TWO
WHY MERE CHRISTIANITY STILL MATTERS

Truth That Refuses to Stay Theoretical

At some point, reflection gives way to reckoning.

Part Two of this book begins where neutrality ends.

Mere Christianity was not written to inspire vague agreement or intellectual admiration. It was written to confront a specific problem: a world that sensed moral obligation but resisted moral authority; a people who spoke of right and wrong but lived as though truth were negotiable; believers who agreed with Christianity without allowing it to change them.

C. S. Lewis wrote *Mere Christianity* after he had already been cornered by truth. What remained was not explanation, but obedience. The book does not ask whether Christianity is interesting. It asks whether it is **true**—and if true, what must follow.

This section turns deliberately toward that question.

The chapters that follow do not summarize *Mere Christianity*. They trace its **pressure points**—the places where belief becomes uncomfortable, where pride is exposed, where self-rule is challenged, and where transformation becomes unavoidable.

Lewis does not soften these moments.

Neither will this book.

Here, Christianity stops being something to evaluate and begins to demand a response. Moral law is no longer abstract. Pride is no longer theoretical. Faith is no longer private. Christ is no longer merely admired.

Part Two prepares you for the journey ahead by clarifying what is at stake.

If Christianity is true, it does not come to improve our behavior.

It comes to remake our selves.

The chapters in this section are meant to narrow the distance between knowing and doing—between understanding and living. They prepare the ground for a 40-day journey that will not ask you merely to think about faith, but to practice it.

Mere Christianity still matters because the problem it addresses has not changed.

Belief is common.

Obedience is rare.

This section exists to make that distinction impossible to ignore.

At some point, reflection gives way to reckoning.

The questions raised in the previous chapters can no longer remain theoretical. Loss has been named. Longing has been awakened. Doubt has been examined. Conscience has spoken. Resistance has been exposed.

What remains is not curiosity, but decision.

The chapters that follow turn directly toward *Mere Christianity*—not as a book to be summarized, but as a truth that presses for response. Here, belief is no longer observed from a distance. It is confronted. Tested. And required to move from agreement into obedience.

This is where neutrality begins to disappear.

CHAPTER SEVEN
Not a Book, but a Reckoning

Why Truth Refuses to Stay Theoretical

When **C. S. Lewis** finally turned toward Christianity, he did not do so as a man seeking comfort. He did so as a man cornered by truth.

Mere Christianity was not written to win arguments or cultivate admiration. It was written because Lewis discovered that belief, once honest, cannot remain neutral. The book exists because the questions Lewis had asked himself would not leave him alone—and because he recognized that those questions pressed on others just as firmly.

At its core, *Mere Christianity* addresses a problem that feels unmistakably modern: people who sense moral obligation, speak of right and wrong, admire Christ, and yet resist the authority that belief implies. Lewis saw that many were willing to accept Christian ideas as long as those ideas did not reorganize life.

That posture troubled him.

Lewis understood that Christianity does not offer itself as one option among many philosophies. It presents itself as a claim about reality—one that, if true, demands response. The faith he had resisted and finally embraced did not come to refine preferences; it came to confront the self.

This is why *Mere Christianity* feels different from other Christian books. It does not flatter the reader. It does not invite agreement without consequence. It moves steadily, almost relentlessly, from recognition to implication.

Lewis begins where resistance is hardest to maintain: with the shared human experience of moral obligation. From there, he presses forward—not to shame, but to clarify. If we know what we ought to do and fail to do it, something is wrong. And if something is wrong at the level of the self, then improvement alone will not suffice.

Christianity, Lewis insists, is not about becoming slightly better people. It is about becoming different people.

This insistence is precisely why *Mere Christianity* still unsettles readers decades later. It leaves little room for compartmentalization. Faith cannot remain private. Belief cannot remain decorative. Christ cannot remain advisory.

The book's power lies not in its complexity, but in its inevitability. Lewis does not rush. He reasons patiently. He allows objections to surface. Yet step by step, he removes the refuge of neutrality. By the time the reader reaches the central claims of Christianity, the question is no longer *Is this interesting?* but *Is this true—and if so, what follows?*

This is why *Mere Christianity* cannot be treated as a mere text to be studied. It is a reckoning.

Lewis knew this because it had first been a reckoning for him. He did not write from a place of superiority, but from experience. The truths he presents are the truths that disrupted his independence, confronted his pride, and demanded his obedience.

And so Part Two of this book turns deliberately toward that confrontation.

The chapters that follow do not summarize *Mere Christianity*. They trace the pressure it applies—the way it exposes pride, redefines freedom, challenges self-rule, and calls for transformation that is both costly and necessary.

If Part One showed how a soul is prepared,

Part Two asks what must now be done.

This is where belief begins to lose its innocence.

And obedience begins to take shape.

INFLECTION POINTS

Questions for Honest Noticing

DO NOT RUSH THESE QUESTIONS.
Let them clarify what is at stake.

1. **What do you typically expect Christian books to give**

you—comfort, clarity, inspiration, or change?
Which of these do you quietly resist?

2. **Have you ever agreed with Christian truth while resisting its implications for your life?**
Where does that tension show up?

3. **In what ways have you allowed belief to remain private or compartmentalized?**
What areas of life feel untouched by faith?

4. **What do you hope Christianity will *not* require of you?**
Sit honestly with that hope.

5. **Do you find yourself more comfortable discussing faith than practicing obedience?**
Why do you think that is?

6. **If Christianity is true, what part of your life can no longer remain neutral?**
Do not act—only notice.

7. **What would it mean for belief to become costly rather than convenient?**
Let that question linger.

Gentle Orientation for the Reader

Truth does not ask to be admired.
It asks to be obeyed.
This chapter does not demand a response yet.
It clarifies why a response will eventually be unavoidable.

CHAPTER EIGHT
The Problem Is Not Behavior, but Selfhood

Why Christianity Does Not Begin With Improvement

One of the most unsettling discoveries **C. S. Lewis** makes in *Mere Christianity* is this:

the central problem Christianity addresses is not what we *do*, but who is in charge of who we *are*.

Most people assume religion exists to make us better behaved. Kinder. More disciplined. More respectable. Lewis dismantles this assumption carefully and relentlessly. Christianity, he argues, is not about helping bad people behave better. It is about transforming people who are fundamentally misaligned at the center.

The issue is not surface-level behavior.

It is **self-rule**.

Lewis observed that many people are willing to make moral adjustments as long as they remain in control. We will change habits, adopt disciplines, and even make sacrifices—provided the self remains sovereign. Christianity, however, does not negotiate with the self. It confronts it.

This is why Christianity feels excessive to modern sensibilities.

We prefer improvement over surrender. We want techniques, not transformation. We ask how much God requires, not who God must become to us. Lewis saw that this posture misunderstands the nature of the faith entirely.

Christianity does not come to make us nicer people.

It comes to make us **new people**.

Lewis uses the image of a house being renovated—not patched, but rebuilt. The walls are not merely repaired; rooms are restructured. Unexpected wings are added. Load-bearing supports are moved. The process is disruptive because the Architect is not interested in cosmetic change.

This is where many resist.

We are often willing to let God correct certain behaviors while protecting the core self from interference. We allow instruction, but resist authority. We accept moral guidance, but not moral ownership. Lewis recognized that this is not Christianity—it is self-improvement with religious language.

The Christian claim goes further: the self that insists on control is the very thing that must be surrendered. Pride, Lewis argues, is not merely one sin among others. It is the condition that keeps all others alive. As long as the self remains enthroned, transformation remains partial.

This is deeply uncomfortable.

It means that Christianity does not leave the self intact. It does not merely advise the ego; it displaces it. Christ does not come to help us run our lives better. He comes to **take over the running of them**.

Lewis knew this personally. His resistance to faith was not primarily intellectual—it was existential. To become a Christian was to relinquish authorship. It was to admit that the self was not qualified to rule itself.

This is where belief often stalls.

We agree with Christian truth while subtly editing its reach. We accept forgiveness but resist formation. We want grace without governance. Lewis refuses this division. Christianity, he insists, either takes the whole self—or it takes nothing.

This is why *Mere Christianity* does not function as a gentle encouragement. It presses toward a conclusion the reader cannot avoid: if Christ is Lord, then the self must step down.

Not improved.

Not advised.

REPLACED AS RULER.

This chapter does not tell you how to do that yet.

It tells you why partial surrender cannot work.

Transformation does not begin with better behavior.

It begins with a change in who is in charge.

INFLECTION POINTS

Questions for Honest Noticing

DO NOT ANSWER DEFENSIVELY.
Let these questions expose posture, not performance.

1. **Where are you most focused on improving behavior rather than yielding control?**
   What feels safer to change?
2. **In what areas of life do you invite God's guidance but resist His authority?**
   Be specific.
3. **How do you react to the idea that Christianity aims to replace self-rule rather than refine it?**
   What emotions surface?
4. **What part of your identity feels most threatened by the idea of surrender?**
   Why do you think that is?
5. **Do you measure spiritual growth more by effort or by alignment?**
   What does that reveal about your posture?
6. **Where might pride be disguising itself as independence or maturity?**
   Sit honestly with that possibility.
7. **If Christ were fully in charge, what would no longer remain negotiable?**
   Do not act—only notice.

Gentle Orientation for the Reader

Christianity does not ask for cooperation.

It asks for surrender.

Not because God is controlling,

but because divided rule cannot heal a divided self.

CHAPTER NINE
The Illusion of Being "Good Enough"

Why Comparison Quietly Resists Grace

One of the quietest barriers to transformation, **C. S. Lewis** observed, is not rebellion—but comparison.

In *Mere Christianity*, Lewis returns repeatedly to a simple but unsettling truth: morality measured by comparison can feel comforting while remaining deeply misleading. As long as we define goodness in relation to others, we can remain at ease without ever being transformed.

Comparison softens conviction.

We reassure ourselves that we are not as dishonest, not as cruel, not as selfish as someone else. We locate righteousness on a sliding scale rather than an objective one. And because someone will always appear worse than us, moral urgency fades.

Lewis recognized how easily this posture embeds itself in religious life.

People who would never claim perfection quietly rely on proximity. They judge their lives against peers, cultures, or extremes rather than against truth. The result is a tolerable conscience—one that feels moral without being surrendered.

Christianity interrupts this comfort.

Lewis insists that Christianity does not ask whether we are better than others, but whether we are aligned with God. The standard is not relative improvement; it is holiness. And holiness does not allow comparison to substitute for transformation.

This is deeply unsettling.

Comparison allows us to remain the judge. Grace removes that role entirely. When comparison governs, we retain control over evaluation. When grace governs, we are exposed—not against others, but against truth itself.

Lewis understood that this exposure feels unfair.

Why should someone outwardly respectable be as dependent on grace as someone visibly broken? Why should quiet pride be treated with the same seriousness as obvious vice? The answer, Lewis argues, is that the problem Christianity addresses is not the *degree* of wrongdoing, but the *condition* of the self.

Relative goodness masks absolute need.

The illusion of being "good enough" delays surrender precisely because it feels reasonable. We acknowledge imperfection without feeling urgency. We accept forgiveness without transformation. We speak of grace while protecting our self-assessments.

Lewis dismantles this illusion patiently. He does not deny moral differences between people, but he refuses to allow those differences to function as refuge. The Christian claim is not that all sins look the same, but that all self-rule resists God.

Comparison keeps the self intact.

Grace, by contrast, leaves no room for self-congratulation. It does not flatter progress; it invites dependence. And dependence is difficult for those who have learned to measure themselves favorably.

This is why *Mere Christianity* feels piercing rather than encouraging at times. It does not allow readers to rest in respectability. It presses toward an uncomfortable conclusion: as long as we ask *"Am I better than others?"* rather than *"Am I yielded to God?"*, transformation will remain partial.

Lewis is not trying to discourage moral effort. He is trying to remove false confidence. Christianity does not level everyone downward; it levels everyone inward—toward honesty, humility, and need.

The illusion of being "good enough" fades only when comparison loses its authority.

This chapter does not condemn moral striving.

It exposes moral comfort.

And it asks whether grace has been received as rescue—or merely as reassurance.

INFLECTION POINTS

Questions for Honest Noticing

LET THESE QUESTIONS unsettle gently.
  They are meant to clarify posture, not performance.

1. **Who do you instinctively compare yourself to when evaluating your spiritual life?**
   Why those people?
2. **How does comparison shape your sense of need for grace?**
   Does it heighten urgency—or soften it?
3. **Where have you accepted forgiveness without allowing it to challenge your self-assessment?**
   Sit with that tension.
4. **Do you find comfort in being "not that bad"?**
   What does that comfort protect?
5. **How do you react to the idea that morality measured by comparison can resist transformation?**
   What emotions surface?
6. **Where might relative goodness be delaying deeper surrender?**
   Be specific.
7. **If comparison were removed, what would grace need to address in you directly?**
   Do not answer—only notice.

Gentle Orientation for the Reader

Grace does not come to reassure the self.

It comes to rescue it.

Comparison makes us comfortable.

Grace makes us honest.

CHAPTER TEN
Counting the Cost of a New Self

Why Transformation Requires Loss Before It Gives Life

By the time **C. S. Lewis** presses deeper into the implications of Christianity, one reality becomes unavoidable: transformation is not additive—it is subtractive before it is restorative.

Christianity does not merely give us something new.

It asks us to relinquish something old.

In *Mere Christianity*, Lewis is unambiguous: becoming a Christian is not about refining the existing self. It is about allowing the old self—the one organized around autonomy, control, and self-justification—to lose its authority.

This is where many hesitate.

We are often drawn to the promises of faith—peace, purpose, forgiveness, renewal—without fully reckoning with the cost. We want transformation without displacement. We hope Christ will strengthen the self rather than replace its rule. Lewis insists this is impossible.

The self cannot remain sovereign and be healed at the same time.

This is not because God is demanding, but because divided authority cannot produce wholeness. A life governed partly by Christ and partly by self-rule remains internally conflicted. Transformation requires coherence, and coherence requires a single center.

Lewis understood how threatening this feels.

To become "new" sounds appealing in theory, but in practice it means losing familiar identities. Patterns of control. Carefully managed narratives about who we are and why we behave as we do. The old self may be flawed, but it is known. The new self requires trust.

This is why surrender feels costly.

Christianity does not negotiate with the ego. It does not promise to preserve our preferred version of ourselves. Lewis famously notes that Christ does not come to improve the old nature; He comes to kill it and give us a new one.

This language is unsettling for modern readers accustomed to self-affirmation. We are taught to protect identity at all costs. Lewis challenges that assumption. He suggests that the self we protect most fiercely is often the self that keeps us from freedom.

Loss, then, is not incidental to transformation.

It is essential.

The cost is not merely behavioral. It is existential. It involves relinquishing the right to define good and evil for ourselves, the right to determine the direction of our lives, the right to remain unchanged while still feeling justified.

Lewis does not minimize this cost. He names it plainly. Christianity will interfere. It will disrupt. It will dismantle familiar structures before rebuilding anything lasting.

Yet Lewis also insists that what is lost is not ultimately what we were meant to keep.

The old self promises control but delivers anxiety.

It promises autonomy but produces fragmentation.

It promises safety but cannot heal.

What Christianity offers in return is not comfort, but life.

Not self-expression, but selfhood rightly ordered.

Not survival, but transformation.

This chapter does not rush the exchange.

It simply clarifies the terms.

Before the new self can emerge, the old self must release its grip.

And that release will feel like loss before it feels like freedom.

INFLECTION POINTS

Questions for Honest Noticing

LET THESE QUESTIONS surface resistance gently.
They are meant to name cost, not resolve it.

1. **What do you fear you would lose if Christ fully reordered your life?**
   Name it honestly.
2. **Which aspects of your identity feel most tied to control or self-definition?**
   Why do those feel essential?
3. **Have you ever desired change while resisting disruption?**
   What did that resistance preserve?
4. **How do you respond to the idea that transformation requires the old self to step down?**
   What emotions surface first?
5. **Where do you prefer Christ to improve rather than replace your way of living?**
   Be specific.
6. **What feels safer—remaining familiar or becoming whole?**
   Sit with that tension.
7. **If loss is part of the path to life, what might need to be released next?**
   Do not act—only notice.

Gentle Orientation for the Reader
Transformation is not painless.
But it is purposeful.
What is surrendered is not destroyed—
it is displaced to make room for life.

CHAPTER ELEVEN
The Risk of Letting Christ Reorder Everything

Why Trust Must Precede Transformation

By the time **C. S. Lewis** confronts the full implications of Christianity, the issue is no longer whether transformation is necessary.

The issue is **whether Christ can be trusted with it.**

In *Mere Christianity*, Lewis makes a claim that feels both reasonable and terrifying: if Christ is Lord, then no part of life remains untouched. Christianity does not rearrange one room at a time at our convenience. It claims the whole house.

This is where trust becomes the decisive question.

Lewis understood that surrender is not merely about loss—it is about **confidence in the One to whom authority is given**. We resist reordering not because we love disorder, but because we fear misplacement. We worry that if Christ takes control, something essential will be lost, silenced, or diminished.

So we hesitate.

We ask whether obedience will erase personality, suppress desire, or flatten joy. We fear becoming less ourselves rather than more. Lewis confronts this fear directly. He insists that Christ does not come to destroy individuality, but to rescue it. The self we protect most fiercely, he argues, is often the self least capable of becoming whole.

This requires a radical shift in imagination.

Trusting Christ means believing that His reordering is wiser than our arrangement. It means allowing Him to touch motives, ambitions, relationships, habits, and identities we have carefully curated. It means admitting that the self has not governed itself as well as it hoped.

This is deeply vulnerable.

Lewis knew that Christianity's demand for trust feels unreasonable precisely because it is total. Partial trust feels safer. Controlled obedience feels manageable. But Christianity does not offer managed transformation. It offers restoration through surrender.

This is where many stall.

We delay not because we doubt Christ's goodness in theory, but because we are unsure we will recognize ourselves after obedience. We fear that yielding will make us smaller, quieter, or less alive.

Lewis insists the opposite is true.

The paradox at the heart of Christianity is that the self is not lost through surrender—it is found. The will that steps down does not disappear; it is healed. The identity that yields is not erased; it is clarified.

But this cannot be proven in advance.

Trust always precedes experience.

Lewis understood that no argument could remove this risk. Christianity does not offer guarantees that can be inspected beforehand. It asks for confidence rooted in truth rather than certainty rooted in control.

This is the final threshold before action.

Not whether Christianity makes sense.

Not whether transformation is needed.

But whether Christ is trustworthy enough to lead.

This chapter does not demand that trust yet.

It asks whether the refusal to trust has become the final barrier.

INFLECTION POINTS

Questions for Honest Noticing

LET THESE QUESTIONS surface fear gently.
They are meant to clarify trust, not force decision.

1. **What do you fear Christ might rearrange if you yielded fully?**
   Name it honestly.
2. **Where do you trust Christ with truth but not with control?**
   What areas remain guarded?
3. **How do you imagine obedience affecting your identity?**
   Smaller? Safer? Diminished? Changed?
4. **What experiences have taught you to associate control with safety?**
   How might those experiences be shaping your resistance?
5. **Do you believe Christ desires your wholeness—or merely your compliance?**
   Why does that distinction matter to you?
6. **Where might mistrust be masquerading as caution or wisdom?**
   Sit with that possibility.
7. **If Christ truly knew you better than you know yourself, what might reordering make possible?**
   Do not answer—only notice.

Gentle Orientation for the Reader
Trust cannot be tested from a distance.
It must be exercised.
Christianity does not ask for blind faith—
but it does ask for surrendered confidence.

CHAPTER TWELVE
A LIFE READ BY ALL

Augustine's **From Reluctant Belief to Willing Obedience**
When Readiness Replaces Resistance

By the end of **C. S. Lewis**'s long resistance to Christianity, the struggle had narrowed to a single point.

The question was no longer whether Christianity was true.

It was whether Lewis was willing to live as though it were.

This is the moment where belief, having done its preparatory work, gives way to obedience. Not dramatic obedience. Not heroic obedience. But *willing* obedience—the quiet consent of the will to step down and allow Christ to lead.

Lewis's conversion did not arrive with fanfare. There was no emotional climax, no public declaration of victory. He described it instead as a reluctant yielding, a recognition that resistance could no longer be sustained honestly. He had not been argued into faith so much as worn down by truth.

And truth had done its work.

Mere Christianity emerges from this interior turning. It is not written by someone who triumphed easily, but by someone who surrendered carefully. Lewis knew from experience that obedience cannot be rushed. It cannot be coerced. It must arise from recognition that neutrality has expired.

This is where readiness matters.

Readiness is not enthusiasm.

It is not certainty.

It is not confidence in one's own strength.

Readiness is the quiet acknowledgment that continuing as before is no longer possible.

Lewis reached this place when he realized that belief without obedience was no longer honest. To admire Christ while resisting His authority was to remain divided. To delay surrender indefinitely was to choose self-rule by default.

And so he yielded—not because he felt powerful, but because resistance had become untenable.

This is a crucial distinction for modern readers.

Obedience does not begin when fear disappears.

It begins when truth becomes unavoidable.

Lewis did not step into faith because he felt ready in every sense. He stepped in because he recognized that the life he had been protecting was no longer defensible. The cost of continued resistance outweighed the cost of surrender.

This is what readiness looks like.

It is not the absence of doubt, but the end of postponement.

Not the certainty of outcomes, but the clarity of direction.

Not the mastery of faith, but the willingness to be led.

This chapter completes the immersion because it names what has been forming quietly throughout the journey: the movement from observation to participation, from reflection to response, from belief as concept to obedience as practice.

Nothing has been demanded of you yet.

Nothing has been assigned.

But something has been clarified.

If Christianity is true, then life cannot remain unchanged.

If Christ is Lord, then the self cannot remain sovereign.

If transformation is possible, then postponement becomes a decision.

The chapters that follow—forty days of deliberate practice—do not exist to pressure you. They exist to **walk with you** through the slow, ordinary acts by which obedience becomes embodied.

This is not where the work ends.

It is where it becomes lived.

You are not being asked to perform.

You are being invited to follow.

INFLECTION POINTS

Questions for Honest Noticing

LET THESE QUESTIONS settle.
> They are meant to clarify readiness, not force action.

1. **What has shifted in you since beginning this journey?**
   Not emotionally—*internally*.
2. **Where has resistance softened, even slightly?**
   What no longer feels as defensible as before?
3. **What would it mean to stop postponing obedience in one area of your life?**
   Do not decide yet—only notice.
4. **How do you distinguish between caution and delay?**
   Where might they overlap?
5. **What version of faith have you outgrown through this process?**
   What no longer fits?
6. **If neutrality were no longer an option, what posture would need to change first?**
   Sit with that.
7. **What would "willing obedience" look like for you—not dramatically, but daily?**
   Let the question remain open.

Gentle Orientation for the Reader
Obedience does not begin with confidence.
It begins with consent.
The journey ahead is not about proving belief.
It is about practicing alignment.

TRANSITION INTO THE 40-DAY JOURNEY

What follows is not a study of ideas, but a formation of life.

The next forty days are structured not to inform you, but to shape you—through Scripture, reflection, action, prayer, and honest examination. Each day invites a small, concrete response, because obedience grows through practice, not intention.

You have not been rushed here.

You have been prepared.

The journey now moves from **understanding** to **embodiment**.

And it begins quietly.

LIVING EPISTLES – 40 Day Devotional Series - 2 Study BEGINS... >>>>>

HOW TO USE THIS BOOK

For Individuals and Groups

This devotional is not designed for speed, volume, or information accumulation.

It is designed for **formation**.

1. USING THIS BOOK AS AN INDIVIDUAL

THIS JOURNEY IS MEANT to be lived slowly, attentively, and honestly.

A. A Daily Rhythm (15–30 Minutes)

EACH DAY IS STRUCTURED to be *entered*, not completed.

Recommended flow:

1. Read Slowly

Do not skim.

Read as though the text is reading you.

2. Enter the Scenario

Do not analyze it.

Imagine yourself within it.

Notice what surfaces—resistance, recognition, or discomfort.

3. Sit With the Question

The questions are not designed for quick answers.

Some are meant to accompany you throughout the day.

4. Practice the Action

Each day includes a small act of obedience.

Do it quietly.

Do not announce it.

Let it shape you.

5. Pray Simply

The prayers are intentionally plain.

Use them as written, or allow them to open your own words before God.

B. Posture for Individual Use

FOR THIS BOOK TO DO its work:

- Read **one day per day only**
- Resist the urge to jump ahead
- Do not seek emotional experiences—seek alignment
- Journal only what is necessary; **obedience matters more than insight**

This book works best when read with restraint.

C. When to Pause

IF A PARTICULAR DAY exposes resistance, conviction, or weariness:

- Remain with that day for an additional 24–48 hours
- Practice the action again
- Allow the truth to settle before moving forward

Spiritual formation is rarely linear.

Do not rush what God is forming.

2. USING THIS BOOK IN A GROUP SETTING

THIS BOOK IS INTENTIONALLY written to function within small groups, discipleship circles, leadership cohorts, and ministry teams.

A. Ideal Group Size

- **4–8 people** is optimal
- Fewer than 4 limits shared witness
- More than 10 limits honesty

THIS IS A **formation space**, not a classroom.

B. Recommended Weekly Rhythm

RATHER THAN MEETING daily, groups are encouraged to move at a weekly pace.

Suggested structure:

- Five devotional days completed individually
- One group meeting for reflection and discernment
- One rest or catch-up day

This rhythm allows obedience to be practiced privately and processed corporately.

C. Group Meeting Structure (60–90 Minutes)

1. OPENING STILLNESS (5 minutes)
No updates.
No discussion.
Allow the room to quiet.

2. Shared Reflection (30 minutes)
Each person answers only:

- *What resisted me this week?*
- *What did God surface?*

No fixing.
No teaching.

3. Scripture and Discernment (20 minutes)

Read the key Scriptures aloud slowly.
Ask together:

- *What fruit is forming?*
- *What alignment is being requested?*

4. Prayer and Declaration (15 minutes)

Pray for obedience, not comfort.
Speak the declarations together.

D. Group Agreements (Very Important)

FOR THIS BOOK TO FUNCTION properly in groups, the following must be agreed upon:

- No correcting one another
- No teaching unless invited
- No advice unless requested
- No sharing outside the group
- No spiritual comparison

This is a protected formation environment, not a debate forum.

3. USING THIS BOOK FOR LEADERSHIP & DISCIPLESHIP

THIS DEVOTIONAL IS particularly effective for:

- Church leadership teams
- Ministry interns
- Emerging leaders
- Mature believers entering new responsibility

A. Leadership Emphasis

LEADERS SHOULD PAY special attention to:

- Days addressing authority, silence, endurance, and restraint
- Scenarios that expose control, visibility, and performance
- Actions that require *obedience through limitation*, not initiative

This book forms **character before capacity**.

B. The Role of the Facilitator

IF YOU ARE GUIDING others through this journey:

- Do not dominate discussion
- Model vulnerability without oversharing
- Allow silence
- Protect the pace

Your role is not to be the expert, but the **guardian of the environment**.

4. WHAT THIS BOOK IS — AND IS NOT

THIS BOOK IS:

- A formation journey
- A discipleship tool
- A mirror for obedience
- A commissioning resource

This book is not:

- A theology textbook
- A motivational devotional
- A quick-read program
- A personality-driven study

It is designed to **leave marks**, not impressions.

5. A FINAL WORD TO READERS

WHETHER YOU WALK THROUGH this book alone or with others, the responsibility is the same:

You are not asked to admire truth.

You are asked to become **legible**.

Read slowly.

Obey quietly.

Live clearly.

The world is reading.

The world is reading.

DAY ONE
When Truth Begins to Press

Recognizing the Moment Neutrality Ends

KEY FOCUS SCRIPTURES

- **2 Corinthians 3:2–3** — *You yourselves are our letter... written not with ink but with the Spirit of the living God.*
- **Hebrews 4:12** — *For the word of God is living and active... discerning the thoughts and intentions of the heart.*
- **John 18:37** — *Everyone who belongs to the truth listens to my voice.*

Scripture Reading (Read Slowly)

Do not rush this reading.

Read as one being addressed, not informed.

"You are our epistle, written in our hearts, known and read by all men."

— 2 Corinthians 3:2

Devotional Reflection

Every journey of obedience begins with a moment when truth becomes personal.

Not dramatic.

Not public.

But unavoidable.

Before **C. S. Lewis** ever spoke publicly of faith, he reached a private realization: neutrality was no longer honest. Truth had pressed too closely to be observed from a distance. What he knew could no longer remain theoretical.

This is where discipleship begins—not with enthusiasm, but with recognition.

Most people delay obedience not because they reject truth, but because they hope it will loosen its grip. We assume there will always be time to respond later, when conditions feel safer, clearer, or more convenient. Yet Scripture reveals that truth does not merely inform us—it *addresses* us.

The Word of God is not static.

It is living.

It searches.

It names intention.

Day 1 is not about action.

It is about *acknowledgment*.

If you have begun this journey, it is because something has already stirred—something has pressed, questioned, unsettled, or invited. This stirring is not accidental. It is the Spirit beginning to write.

You are not here to consume content.

You are here to be formed.

Before obedience takes shape, honesty must take root.

Heart Examination

Sit with these questions quietly.

Do not rush to answer them.

1. **What truth has been pressing on you lately that you have not yet responded to?**
2. **Where have you remained neutral even though clarity has already come?**
3. **What do you sense God may be asking you to *acknowledge* before He asks you to *act*?**

Today's Practice (Small but Intentional)

Today's practice is **stillness**.

Set aside **10 uninterrupted minutes**.

No phone. No music. No journal.

Sit quietly before God and say only this—out loud or silently:

"Lord, I am listening."

Do not explain.

Do not negotiate.

Do not plan ahead.

Let truth press without resistance.

Prayer

Father,

I acknowledge that You are not distant.

Your Word is alive, and it searches me.

I surrender my need to stay neutral.

Teach me to listen before I act

and to receive before I respond.

Write Your truth into my life

until my obedience becomes visible.

Amen.

Declaration

Speak this aloud slowly:

I am a living epistle of Christ.

I do not resist truth when it comes close.

I choose honesty over delay

and listening over neutrality.

My life is being written by the Spirit of God.

Commitment to Obedience

Today, I commit not to rush ahead.

I commit to **stay present**.

I commit to letting truth speak

before I attempt to respond.

CLOSING ORIENTATION

Do not move ahead yet.

Let this day settle.

Obedience begins with attention.

Tomorrow, we will examine **why resistance often hides beneath good intentions.**

DAY TWO
When Resistance Wears a Reasonable Face

How Good Intentions Delay Obedience

K EY FOCUS SCRIPTURES

- **Matthew 7:15–20** — *You will recognize them by their fruits.*
- **James 1:22** — *Be doers of the word, and not hearers only, deceiving yourselves.*
- **Luke 9:57–62** — *No one who puts a hand to the plow and looks back is fit for the kingdom of God.*

Scripture Reading (Read Slowly)
"Why do you call me 'Lord, Lord,' and do not do what I tell you?"
— Luke 6:46
Read again.
Let the question stand without answering it yet.
Devotional Reflection
Resistance rarely announces itself as rebellion.
More often, it disguises itself as *reasonableness*.
Before **C. S. Lewis** ever openly rejected Christianity, he delayed it with logic, timing, and sincerity. He did not say "no" outright. He said, *"not yet," "not like this,"* or *"not until I understand more."* These responses felt honest—and they were—but they also functioned as shields.
This is one of the most subtle forms of self-deception.
We assume that because our reasons sound thoughtful, they must be faithful. We confuse explanation with obedience. We mistake reflection for response. Scripture warns us gently but clearly: hearing without doing can

become a form of deception—not intentional hypocrisy, but unexamined delay.

Jesus does not rebuke people for asking questions.

He rebukes them for avoiding alignment.

Day 2 invites you to notice where resistance may have learned to sound wise in your life. Where obedience has been postponed under the banner of discernment. Where good intentions have taken the place of yielded action.

Fruit reveals allegiance.

Time reveals truth.

If something has been pressing on your heart for a long time, the issue may no longer be clarity—it may be consent.

Heart Examination

Sit quietly with these questions.

Let them surface patterns, not answers.

1. **Where have you said "yes" in principle but "later" in practice?**
2. **What reasons do you most often give for delaying obedience?**
3. **How do you distinguish between discernment and avoidance in your own life?**

Today's Practice (Small but Honest)

Today's practice is **naming**.

Take a sheet of paper or a note on your phone.

Write down **one area** where you sense God has already spoken—but you have delayed responding.

Do not justify it.

Do not explain it.

Just name it.

Then say this quietly:

"Lord, I see where I have delayed."

That is all.

Prayer

Lord Jesus,

I confess that resistance does not always look like rebellion.

Sometimes it looks like patience, caution, or wisdom.

Search me and reveal where delay has replaced obedience.

Teach me to recognize fruit rather than excuses

and alignment rather than intention.

I choose honesty over self-protection.

Amen.

Declaration

Speak this aloud:

I do not confuse intention with obedience.

I do not hide resistance behind reason.

I am learning to recognize delay

and to choose alignment with truth.

My life will bear fruit that reflects surrender.

Commitment to Obedience

Today, I commit to **honest recognition**.

I will not rename delay as discernment.

I will allow God to expose what needs alignment

before asking for new direction.

Closing Orientation

Do not act on what you named yet.

Today was about **seeing clearly**, not fixing quickly.

Tomorrow, we will examine **why obedience often feels risky even when truth is clear**.

DAY THREE
When Obedience Feels Risky

Why Clarity Does Not Always Lead to Action

KEY FOCUS SCRIPTURES

- **Proverbs 3:5–6** — *Trust in the Lord with all your heart...*
- **Matthew 14:28–31** — *Peter walked on the water... and began to sink.*
- **Hebrews 11:8** — *By faith Abraham obeyed... not knowing where he was going.*

Scripture Reading (Read Slowly)
"Trust in the Lord with all your heart,
and do not lean on your own understanding."
— Proverbs 3:5
Pause.
Notice where trust—not knowledge—is emphasized.

Devotional Reflection
One of the most misunderstood aspects of obedience is this:
obedience rarely feels *safe* at the moment it is required.

Before **C. S. Lewis** yielded fully to Christianity, he already knew much of what obedience would involve. His resistance was not rooted in ignorance. It was rooted in *risk*. Obedience threatened his sense of control, predictability, and self-authorship.

This is still true for many today.

We often assume that once truth is clear, action should be easy. Scripture tells a different story. Clarity does not remove fear. In fact, clarity often intensifies it—because now the cost is visible.

80

Obedience requires trust at the precise moment when outcomes are unknown.

Peter did not sink because he doubted Jesus existed.

He sank because fear redirected his attention.

Abraham did not obey because he had a map.

He obeyed because he trusted the One who called him.

Day 3 invites you to see that hesitation is not always rebellion—it is often fear of loss, exposure, or change. Obedience asks us to step forward before safety is guaranteed. It requires faith not as confidence in outcome, but as confidence in God's character.

This is where many pause indefinitely.

We wait for certainty when God asks for trust.

We wait for assurance when God asks for alignment.

We wait for clarity about the future when God asks for obedience in the present.

Obedience feels risky because it removes the illusion of control.

Yet Scripture consistently reveals that faith is not the absence of fear—it is movement *through* it.

Heart Examination

Sit with these questions without rushing.

1. **What aspect of obedience currently feels most risky to you?**
2. **What outcome are you trying to protect yourself from?**
3. **How do you usually respond when God asks for movement before certainty?**

Today's Practice (Small but Courageous)

Today's practice is **trust-oriented prayer**.

Find a quiet place.

Name **one specific fear** related to obedience.

Then pray this sentence slowly, three times:

"Lord, I trust You more than the outcome I fear."

Do not argue with the fear.

Do not eliminate it.

Just place trust beside it.

Prayer

Father,

You know where obedience feels costly to me.

You see the fear beneath my hesitation.

Teach me to trust Your character

when I cannot predict the result.

I choose faith that moves forward,

even while fear is still present.

Amen.

Declaration

Speak this aloud:

I do not wait for certainty to obey.

I trust the One who calls me forward.

Fear does not rule my decisions.

Faith leads me step by step.

My obedience grows stronger than my hesitation.

Commitment to Obedience

Today, I commit to **trusting God's character**

even when the outcome remains unclear.

I will not confuse fear with wisdom

or delay with discernment.

Closing Orientation

Do not rush ahead.

Today was about **naming fear**, not conquering it.

Tomorrow, we will explore **how pride subtly resists obedience while appearing responsible**.

DAY FOUR
When Pride Sounds Responsible

How Self-Rule Disguises Itself as Wisdom

KEY FOCUS SCRIPTURES

- **Proverbs 16:18** — *Pride goes before destruction...*
- **Luke 18:9–14** — *The Pharisee and the tax collector.*
- **Romans 12:3** — *Do not think of yourself more highly than you ought...*

Scripture Reading (Read Slowly)
"God opposes the proud
but gives grace to the humble."
— James 4:6
Read again.
Notice the word *opposes*.

Devotional Reflection
Not all pride is loud.
Some pride sounds careful.
Measured.
Responsible.

Before **C. S. Lewis** surrendered to Christ, one of the strongest forms of resistance he faced was not arrogance—but *self-trust*. He believed he was being reasonable, thoughtful, and disciplined. And he was. But beneath that posture was a deeper assumption: *I am capable of governing myself.*

This is one of pride's most convincing disguises.

We often imagine pride as boasting or self-importance. Scripture reveals something more subtle: pride is the insistence that *I know best how to manage my life*. It is self-rule presented as maturity. Control presented as caution. Independence presented as wisdom.

Lewis recognized that as long as he remained the final authority, Christianity could not take root fully. He could accept moral guidance, appreciate Christian teaching, and even admire Christ—while still retaining control over what obedience would look like.

Pride does not always reject God.

It often negotiates with Him.

It agrees in principle while resisting surrender in practice. It prefers consultation over submission. It accepts help without yielding authority. And because it feels sensible, it often goes unchallenged.

Jesus addresses this directly in His parables. The Pharisee in Luke 18 does not appear immoral. He appears responsible. Upright. Religious. Yet his posture leaves no room for grace, because it leaves no room for need.

Grace cannot land where self-sufficiency remains intact.

Day 4 invites you to notice where obedience may be resisted not through defiance, but through self-confidence. Where reliance on your own judgment quietly competes with trust in God's direction.

This is not about condemning competence or responsibility.

It is about recognizing when they have replaced dependence.

Pride rarely announces itself as rebellion.

It whispers, *"I've got this."*

Heart Examination

Sit quietly with these questions.

1. **Where do you rely most on your own judgment rather than God's leading?**
2. **How do you respond when obedience feels inefficient or impractical?**
3. **What does humility look like in areas where you feel most competent?**

Today's Practice (Small but Revealing)

Today's practice is **release**.

Identify **one decision, habit, or area of life** you manage entirely on your own.

Pray this sentence slowly:

"Lord, I release my need to control this."

Do not fix it.

Do not improve it.

Just release it into God's care.

Prayer

Father,

I confess that pride does not always feel sinful.

Sometimes it feels wise, careful, and strong.

Show me where self-rule has replaced trust.

Teach me humility that receives grace

and obedience that flows from dependence.

I step down so You may lead.

Amen.

Declaration

Speak this aloud:

I do not rely on my own understanding.

I yield my competence to God's wisdom.

Pride does not guide my decisions.

Grace shapes my obedience.

I choose humility over control.

Commitment to Obedience

Today, I commit to **releasing self-rule**.

I will not confuse responsibility with independence

or wisdom with control.

I choose trust over self-sufficiency.

Closing Orientation

Do not rush to correct anything today.

Today was about **recognizing posture**, not producing change.

Tomorrow, we will confront **how partial obedience creates inner conflict**

DAY FIVE

When Obedience Is Partial

Why Divided Allegiance Creates Inner Conflict

KEY FOCUS SCRIPTURES

- **1 Kings 18:21** — *How long will you waver between two opinions?*
- **Luke 9:23** — *Whoever wants to be my disciple must deny themselves...*
- **Romans 7:22–25** — *I delight in God's law... but I see another law at work in me.*

Scripture Reading (Read Slowly)
"No one can serve two masters."
— Matthew 6:24
Pause.
Do not explain the verse away.
Let it stand.

Devotional Reflection
Partial obedience feels reasonable.

It allows us to say yes without surrendering everything. It lets us follow Christ in visible ways while quietly reserving certain areas for ourselves. And because partial obedience often looks sincere, it can persist for years without being confronted.

Before **C. S. Lewis** fully yielded to Christ, he lived in this tension. He admired Christian truth, accepted its moral clarity, and even acknowledged its authority—yet he delayed full surrender. His life was not marked by open rebellion, but by divided allegiance.

This division creates strain.

Scripture does not describe inner conflict as a mystery. It names it as the result of competing authorities. When Christ governs some areas and the self governs others, peace remains elusive. Not because God withholds it—but because divided rule cannot sustain wholeness.

Partial obedience exhausts us.

We carry the weight of decision-making while attempting to follow Christ. We manage faith rather than receive guidance. We oscillate between trust and control, obedience and reservation. And the result is often fatigue, frustration, and a quiet sense that something is misaligned.

God does not expose this tension to shame us.

He reveals it to invite us into rest.

Rest is not found in doing less for God, but in yielding more to Him.

Lewis eventually recognized that Christianity does not function under shared leadership. Christ does not negotiate authority; He assumes it. The peace Lewis sought did not arrive through incremental adjustment, but through relinquished control.

Day 5 invites you to notice where obedience may be sincere but incomplete. Where Christ is welcomed as Savior but resisted as Lord. Where faith has been divided to preserve comfort, control, or familiarity.

This recognition is not failure.

It is progress.

Inner conflict often signals that alignment is near.

Heart Examination

Sit with these questions quietly.

1. **Where have you offered obedience with conditions attached?**
2. **What area of life feels most resistant to full surrender?**
3. **How does partial obedience show up emotionally—in fatigue, frustration, or restlessness?**

Today's Practice (Small but Clarifying)

Today's practice is **honest inventory**.

Write down **three areas** of your life:

- One where obedience feels natural
- One where obedience feels selective
- One where obedience feels resisted

Do not judge what you write.
Just notice the pattern.
Then say quietly:
"Lord, show me where my allegiance is divided."

Prayer

Lord Jesus,
I confess that I have often offered You partial obedience.
I have followed You where it felt safe
and resisted You where it felt costly.
Reveal where division has replaced surrender.
Teach me the peace that comes from wholeness,
not from control.
I choose alignment over negotiation.
Amen.

Declaration

Speak this aloud:
I do not serve divided masters.
I choose wholeness over control.
My obedience is not partial or conditional.
Christ is Lord over every area of my life.
I receive peace through surrender.

Commitment to Obedience

Today, I commit to **honest awareness**.

I will no longer ignore areas of divided allegiance.

I choose alignment as the path to rest.

Closing Orientation

Let today settle.

Do not rush to correct everything at once.

Tomorrow, we will explore **why obedience must be practiced daily—not decided once.**

DAY SIX
Obedience Is Learned Daily

Why Alignment Is Practiced, Not Decided Once

KEY FOCUS SCRIPTURES

- **Luke 9:23** — *Take up your cross daily and follow Me.*
- **Lamentations 3:22–23** — *His mercies are new every morning.*
- **Philippians 2:12–13** — *Work out your salvation... for it is God who works in you.*

Scripture Reading (Read Slowly)

"Whoever wants to be my disciple must deny themselves and take up their cross daily and follow me."
— Luke 9:23

Notice the word **daily**.

Do not spiritualize it away.

Devotional Reflection

One of the quiet misconceptions about obedience is the belief that it can be settled once and for all.

We imagine a decisive moment—a prayer, a commitment, a breakthrough—after which obedience becomes automatic. But Scripture consistently presents obedience not as a single event, but as a **daily posture**.

Before **C. S. Lewis** became a public Christian voice, his surrender unfolded gradually. His resistance did not collapse in one dramatic act; it loosened

through repeated, ordinary choices to align with truth as it presented itself. Obedience became learned through rhythm, not resolve.

This is deeply freeing.

If obedience were sustained by intensity, most would fail quickly. Instead, God forms obedience through repetition—through returning each day to the same decision: *Who is in charge today?*

Daily obedience acknowledges something honest about us:

we wake up each morning with the self still eager to rule.

This is not failure.

It is reality.

Scripture does not ask us to crucify the self once.

It asks us to take up the cross **daily**.

Day 6 invites you to release the pressure of perfection and embrace the discipline of presence. Obedience grows not through heroic effort, but through repeated consent. Each day becomes a new opportunity to realign—not because yesterday was insufficient, but because today brings its own choices.

God's mercy meets us there.

Daily obedience does not demand that we feel committed.

It asks that we remain available.

It does not require foresight.

It requires faithfulness in the present moment.

This is how transformation becomes sustainable.

Heart Examination

Sit with these questions quietly.

1. **Where do you expect obedience to be settled once rather than practiced daily?**
2. **How do you typically respond when yesterday's clarity feels distant today?**
3. **What would it look like to approach obedience as a daily return rather than a permanent state?**

TODAY'S PRACTICE (SIMPLE and Repeatable)

Today's practice is **daily consent**.
At the start of your day—or right now—say this slowly:
"Lord, I choose alignment today."
Do not add conditions.
Do not project into tomorrow.
Let obedience remain present-tense.

Prayer
Father,
Thank You that obedience is formed over time.
Release me from the pressure to resolve everything at once.
Teach me faithfulness in today's choices
and trust in Your mercy for tomorrow.
I offer You this day—
not perfectly, but willingly.
Amen.

Declaration
Speak this aloud:
Obedience is formed daily in my life.
I do not rely on yesterday's resolve.
I choose alignment today.
God's grace meets me in repetition.
My faith grows through faithful practice.

Commitment to Obedience
Today, I commit to **present obedience**.
I will not demand certainty for tomorrow
before yielding today.
I choose daily alignment over delayed perfection.

Closing Orientation
Let today be light.
You are learning a rhythm, not proving devotion.
Tomorrow, we will explore **why obedience deepens through small, hidden choices rather than visible ones.**

DAY SEVEN
Faithfulness in the Hidden Places

Why Obedience Grows Where No One Sees

K EY FOCUS SCRIPTURES

- **Matthew 6:1–6** — *Your Father who sees in secret will reward you.*
- **Luke 16:10** — *Whoever is faithful in very little is faithful also in much.*
- **Colossians 3:23–24** — *Whatever you do, work at it with all your heart, as working for the Lord.*

Scripture Reading (Read Slowly)
"Your Father, who sees what is done in secret, will reward you."
— Matthew 6:4
Pause.
Notice who the audience is.

Devotional Reflection
Much of obedience happens where it cannot be measured.

Before **C. S. Lewis** ever spoke publicly about Christianity, his obedience was being shaped in unseen ways. His surrender did not begin on a platform or in print. It unfolded in private alignment—choices no one applauded, adjustments no one noticed, faithfulness that produced no immediate recognition.

This is where obedience grows strongest.

We often associate obedience with visible acts—public faith, moral stands, courageous decisions. Scripture reveals something quieter: God forms character in hidden places. What we do when no one is watching shapes who we become when everyone is.

Hidden obedience tests motive.

It asks whether we follow Christ for recognition or for alignment. Whether we obey for reward or for faithfulness. Whether our allegiance depends on affirmation or remains steady in obscurity.

Lewis understood this deeply. His early obedience did not make him famous. It made him faithful. Long before his writings influenced millions, his choices shaped a life ordered toward truth. The fruit came later. The formation came first.

This is especially challenging in a culture that rewards visibility.

We are tempted to measure progress by noticeability. We equate growth with affirmation. Yet Jesus consistently redirects attention away from the crowd and toward the Father who sees in secret.

Day 7 invites you to reframe obedience not as performance, but as presence.

Hidden obedience is not wasted.

It is weighted.

It prepares us to carry responsibility without corruption, influence without pride, and fruit without entitlement. Faithfulness in secret forms the spine of public integrity.

If you feel unseen in your obedience, you are not behind.

You are being formed.

Heart Examination

Sit with these questions quietly.

1. **What acts of obedience in your life remain unseen by others?**
2. **How do you respond emotionally when faithfulness goes unnoticed?**
3. **What motivates your obedience most—alignment or affirmation?**

Today's Practice (Quiet and Intentional)

Today's practice is **secret obedience**.

Choose **one small act of faithfulness** that no one else will know about:

- A prayer
- An act of restraint
- A moment of generosity
- A decision to speak kindly or remain silent

Do it quietly.
Do not record it.
Do not mention it.
Let it be between you and God.

Prayer
Father,
You see what is done in secret.
Teach me to value Your gaze over recognition.
Form my obedience where applause is absent
and faithfulness must stand on its own.
I offer You what no one else will see.
Amen.

Declaration
Speak this aloud:
My obedience is not performative.
I am faithful where no one sees.
God forms my character in hidden places.
I live for alignment, not applause.
My faithfulness bears fruit in due season.

Commitment to Obedience
Today, I commit to **hidden faithfulness**.
I choose obedience without recognition
and alignment without affirmation.

CLOSING ORIENTATION
This completes **Week One**.
You have not been asked to do much—
but much has been quietly happening.

Next week, we will explore **how obedience reshapes desire, not just behavior.**

DAY EIGHT
When Desire Begins to Change

How Obedience Reorders What We Love

KEY FOCUS SCRIPTURES

- **Psalm 37:4** — *Delight yourself in the Lord, and He will give you the desires of your heart.*
- **Ezekiel 36:26** — *I will give you a new heart and put a new spirit within you.*
- **Galatians 5:16–17** — *Walk by the Spirit, and you will not gratify the desires of the flesh.*

Scripture Reading (Read Slowly)
"I will give you a new heart,
and put a new spirit within you."
— Ezekiel 36:26
Notice that God does not begin with behavior.
He begins with **the heart**.

Devotional Reflection
Many people assume that obedience suppresses desire.

They imagine faith as restraint—doing what is right while longing for something else. This misunderstanding causes obedience to feel heavy and temporary. Yet Scripture reveals a deeper truth: obedience does not merely restrain desire; it **reshapes it**.

Before **C. S. Lewis** experienced lasting freedom in Christ, he learned that Christian transformation was not about overpowering desire through willpower. It was about allowing desire itself to be reordered. What once pulled him away from God began, slowly, to lose its authority.

This does not happen instantly.

Desire changes gradually—through repeated alignment, through choosing obedience even when desire lags behind. Over time, what once felt costly begins to feel natural. What once required effort begins to bring peace.

This is not repression.

It is renewal.

God does not ask us to pretend our desires are different than they are. He promises to *make them different*. But that promise unfolds through practice, not pressure. As we walk in obedience, the Spirit reshapes our loves from the inside out.

Day 8 invites you to notice subtle shifts.

You may not yet want everything God asks.

But you may begin to want *alignment itself*.

And that is where change begins.

Christian maturity is not marked by the absence of desire, but by the transformation of it.

Heart Examination

Sit with these questions quietly.

1. **What desires currently compete with obedience in your life?**
2. **Have you noticed any desires losing their pull since beginning this journey?**
3. **What would it mean to trust God with the reshaping of your desires, not just your actions?**

Today's Practice (Gentle and Observational)

Today's practice is **noticing desire**.

Throughout the day, pause once or twice and ask yourself:

"What am I wanting right now?"

Do not judge the desire.

Do not correct it.

Just notice it.

Then quietly pray:

"Lord, shape what I love."

Prayer

Father,

You know my desires better than I do.

I bring them to You without pretending or hiding.

Shape my heart from the inside out.

Let obedience become something I desire,

not merely something I perform.

I trust You with my loves.

Amen.

Declaration

Speak this aloud:

God is reshaping my desires.

Obedience is becoming my delight.

I walk by the Spirit, not by impulse.

My heart is being renewed daily.

What I love is coming into alignment with truth.

Commitment to Obedience

Today, I commit to **honest awareness of desire**.

I will not fear my longings

or pretend they do not exist.

I trust God to reorder them over time.

Closing Orientation

Do not measure today by feeling.

Measure it by **attention**.

Desire changes quietly.

Tomorrow, we will explore **why obedience matures through patience, not urgency**.

DAY NINE
The Quiet Work of Patience

Why Obedience Matures Over Time

K EY FOCUS SCRIPTURES

- **James 1:2–4** — *Let perseverance finish its work so that you may be mature and complete.*
- **Galatians 6:9** — *Let us not grow weary in doing good...*
- **Psalm 40:1** — *I waited patiently for the Lord; He turned to me and heard my cry.*

Scripture Reading (Read Slowly)
"Let perseverance finish its work
so that you may be mature and complete,
lacking nothing."
— James 1:4
Notice that maturity is something **allowed**, not forced.

Devotional Reflection
Obedience often falters not because it is rejected—but because it is rushed.

We want clarity quickly. Change quickly. Resolution quickly. And when progress feels slow, we assume something is wrong. Yet Scripture consistently reveals that God works **deliberately**, not urgently. He forms maturity over time, not through acceleration.

Before **C. S. Lewis** became a trusted Christian voice, much of his formation happened quietly, without visible milestones. His obedience unfolded through patience—through allowing truth to do its work rather than demanding immediate results.

101

This is difficult for modern readers.

We live in a culture of immediacy. We expect transformation to be measurable, fast, and emotionally affirming. But spiritual formation resists efficiency. God is not in a hurry to produce outcomes; He is committed to producing *wholeness*.

Patience protects obedience.

When we rush obedience, we often substitute activity for alignment. We do more instead of yielding more. We pursue momentum instead of maturity. Over time, this leads to weariness rather than fruit.

Scripture invites a different posture: perseverance that allows God's work to finish.

This does not mean passivity.

It means *faithful presence*.

Patience in obedience teaches us to remain aligned even when results are unseen. It trains us to trust God's timing rather than manipulate outcomes. It deepens roots so that future fruit can be sustained.

Day 9 invites you to release the pressure to be "further along." Growth is happening even when it feels imperceptible. Obedience matures not by intensity, but by consistency.

Waiting is not wasted when God is at work.

Heart Examination

Sit with these questions quietly.

1. **Where do you feel pressure to progress faster than you are?**
2. **How do you respond when obedience feels repetitive or slow?**
3. **What might patience be protecting in your spiritual formation right now?**

Today's Practice (Slow and Intentional)

Today's practice is **unhurried faithfulness**.

Choose **one ordinary act of obedience** you already practice—prayer, kindness, restraint, honesty.

Do it today **without trying to improve it**.

Simply do it faithfully.

Then pray:

"Lord, I trust Your timing."

Prayer

Father,

Teach me to value faithfulness over speed.

Release me from the pressure to rush Your work.

Help me remain steady when growth feels slow

and patient when results are unseen.

I trust You to finish what You have begun.

Amen.

Declaration

Speak this aloud:

I do not rush God's work in my life.

Obedience matures through patience.

I remain faithful in the ordinary.

God completes His work in His time.

I grow steady, rooted, and whole.

Commitment to Obedience

Today, I commit to **patient alignment**.

I will not measure progress by speed

or judge growth by visibility.

I trust God to finish His work in me.

Closing Orientation

Let today be slow.

Maturity grows quietly.

Tomorrow, we will examine **how obedience reshapes our response to temptation—not by avoidance, but by formation.**

.

DAY TEN
When Temptation Reveals Formation

Why Obedience Changes How We Respond, Not Just What We Resist

KEY FOCUS SCRIPTURES

- **1 Corinthians 10:13** — *God is faithful; He will not let you be tempted beyond what you can bear.*
- **James 1:13–15** — *Each person is tempted when they are dragged away by their own desire...*
- **Galatians 5:24–25** — *Those who belong to Christ Jesus have crucified the flesh...*

Scripture Reading (Read Slowly)

"Each person is tempted when they are dragged away by their own desire and enticed."

— James 1:14

Notice where temptation begins.

Not outside—but within.

Devotional Reflection

Temptation is often misunderstood.

We treat it as an external threat—something to avoid, suppress, or escape. Scripture presents a deeper truth: temptation reveals what is still being formed inside us. It exposes the desires, habits, and reflexes that obedience is gradually reshaping.

Before **C. S. Lewis** learned to speak clearly about Christian transformation, he learned this personally. Temptation did not disappear after belief; it changed character as obedience deepened. What once felt overpowering slowly lost its authority—not through avoidance alone, but through reordered desire.

This is important.

Victory over temptation is not primarily about stronger willpower. It is about a transformed will. As obedience matures, temptation is met not with panic, but with clarity. The pull weakens because the heart is being redirected.

Temptation does not mean failure.

It means formation is still underway.

Scripture does not shame us for being tempted. It invites us to examine what temptation reveals. Where desire remains unformed, temptation feels urgent. Where desire is being reshaped, temptation feels exposed.

Day 10 invites you to stop treating temptation as an emergency and begin seeing it as information.

What you are tempted by reveals what still competes for allegiance. And that awareness is not condemnation—it is guidance. God uses even temptation to show us where obedience is still taking root.

This reframing changes everything.

Instead of fearing temptation, we learn from it.

Instead of hiding it, we examine it.

Instead of fighting blindly, we align deliberately.

Obedience does not make us immune.

It makes us attentive.

Heart Examination

Sit with these questions quietly.

1. **What patterns of temptation recur most often in your life?**
2. **What desires do those temptations reveal?**
3. **How has your response to temptation changed—if at all—since beginning this journey?**

TODAY'S PRACTICE (REFLECTIVE and Grounding)

Today's practice is **examined response**.

When you notice temptation today—small or large—pause and ask:

"What is this revealing about what I still desire?"
Then pray quietly:
"Lord, continue reshaping my heart."
Do not shame yourself.
Do not rush away.
Just learn.

Prayer

Father,
Thank You that temptation does not disqualify me.
Teach me to see it as a mirror, not a verdict.
Reveal what still competes for my allegiance,
and continue reshaping my desires through obedience.
I trust Your faithfulness in every test.
Amen.

Declaration

Speak this aloud:
Temptation does not define me.
God is forming my heart through obedience.
I walk by the Spirit, not by impulse.
My desires are being reshaped by truth.
I grow in clarity and freedom each day.

Commitment to Obedience

Today, I commit to **attentive obedience**.
I will not fear temptation
or hide from what it reveals.
I allow God to use every moment
to continue forming my heart.

CLOSING ORIENTATION

You are not behind.
You are being shaped.
Tomorrow, we will explore **how obedience strengthens through community rather than isolation.**

DAY ELEVEN
Obedience Grows in Community

Why Formation Was Never Meant to Be Private

KEY FOCUS SCRIPTURES

- **Hebrews 10:24–25** — *Let us consider how to stir up one another to love and good works.*
- **Ecclesiastes 4:9–12** — *Two are better than one... a cord of three strands is not quickly broken.*
- **Proverbs 27:17** — *As iron sharpens iron, so one person sharpens another.*

Scripture Reading (Read Slowly)
"Let us consider how to stir up one another to love and good works."
— Hebrews 10:24
Notice the word **consider**.
Community requires intention.
Devotional Reflection
One of the quiet myths of modern faith is the idea that obedience can be sustained alone.

We value privacy. Independence. Personal spirituality. While these can be gifts, they easily become liabilities when they isolate us from correction, encouragement, and shared discernment. Scripture never presents obedience as a solo endeavor. Formation, by design, is communal.

Before **C. S. Lewis** became known for his public writings, his obedience was sharpened in friendship. Conversations, disagreements, accountability, and shared pursuit of truth shaped his faith. Lewis did not arrive at maturity alone;

he was formed among others who challenged, questioned, and walked with him.

Community exposes blind spots.

Left alone, we justify delay. We normalize partial obedience. We confuse sincerity with alignment. Community interrupts these patterns—not through judgment, but through presence. Others see what we cannot. They name what we avoid. They remind us of truth when our resolve weakens.

This does not mean constant sharing or forced vulnerability. It means *shared direction*. Walking toward the same center. Allowing our lives to be known enough to be shaped.

Day 11 invites you to reconsider how obedience functions in your life.

Where faith remains isolated, it often becomes fragile.

Where obedience is shared, it becomes resilient.

Community does not replace personal responsibility.

It strengthens it.

God uses others to steady our steps, to correct our drift, and to remind us that obedience is not merely an individual achievement—it is a shared witness.

Heart Examination

Sit with these questions quietly.

1. **Where do you tend to isolate your faith from others?**
2. **How do you typically respond to correction or challenge?**
3. **Who knows enough about your life to encourage your obedience honestly?**

Today's Practice (Relational and Intentional)

Today's practice is **intentional connection**.

Reach out to **one trusted person**—a friend, mentor, or fellow believer.

You do not need to explain everything.

Simply say something like:

"I'm being more intentional about alignment in my life. Please pray for me."

Let obedience be *seen*, even briefly.

Prayer

Father,

You did not design me to walk alone.

Teach me to receive strength through community
and humility through shared pursuit of truth.
Help me welcome encouragement and correction
as gifts that protect my obedience.
I choose connection over isolation.
Amen.

Declaration

Speak this aloud:
I am not formed alone.
God strengthens my obedience through community.
I welcome encouragement and correction.
My faith grows resilient through shared pursuit of truth.
I walk in alignment with others.

Commitment to Obedience

Today, I commit to **shared obedience**.
I will not isolate what God is forming.
I choose connection as a safeguard for alignment.

Closing Orientation

Let today remind you:
obedience is not a private achievement.
Tomorrow, we will explore **how obedience reshapes the way we handle failure and weakness**.

DAY TWELVE
When Obedience Meets Weakness

How Failure Becomes a Place of Formation

K EY FOCUS SCRIPTURES

- **2 Corinthians 12:9–10** — *My grace is sufficient for you, for my power is made perfect in weakness.*
- **Psalm 51:16–17** — *A broken and contrite heart, O God, you will not despise.*
- **Proverbs 24:16** — *Though the righteous fall seven times, they rise again.*

Scripture Reading (Read Slowly)
"My grace is sufficient for you,
for my power is made perfect in weakness."
— 2 Corinthians 12:9
Pause.
Notice that grace meets weakness—not strength.

Devotional Reflection
One of the most dangerous misunderstandings about obedience is the belief that failure disqualifies us from it.

Many believers assume that obedience must be uninterrupted to be authentic. When weakness surfaces—when resolve falters, when temptation wins, when alignment slips—we retreat in shame. We interpret failure as evidence that formation has stopped.

Scripture tells a different story.

Before becoming a trusted Christian voice, **C. S. Lewis** learned that weakness did not end obedience—it revealed where grace was still forming him. Christianity, as Lewis understood it, does not depend on our consistency but on God's faithfulness. Obedience is not sustained by strength alone; it is sustained by *returning*.

Failure exposes what remains unhealed.

It shows us where self-reliance still operates, where humility is still needed, where grace has not yet been fully received. God does not use failure to condemn us. He uses it to invite deeper dependence.

This is why Scripture speaks so honestly about falling.

The righteous fall—not once, but repeatedly. What distinguishes them is not perfection, but response. They rise again because grace restores what pride would abandon.

Day 12 invites you to reframe weakness.

Weakness is not proof that obedience is impossible.

It is proof that obedience must be sustained by grace.

When we hide failure, obedience becomes performative.

When we bring failure into the light, obedience becomes honest.

Lewis understood that Christianity does not produce flawless people. It produces repentant ones. People who do not defend their weakness, but surrender it. People who do not pretend to be strong, but learn to rely on grace.

This is how obedience deepens.

Not through avoiding weakness,

but through meeting it with humility.

Heart Examination

Sit with these questions quietly.

1. **How do you typically respond when you fall short?**
   With shame, denial, determination—or return?
2. **What weakness in your life feels most discouraging right now?**
3. **How might God be inviting you to depend more deeply on grace rather than effort?**

Today's Practice (Restorative and Honest)

Today's practice is **return**.

Identify **one recent failure or area of weakness**—small or significant.
Bring it to God plainly.
No explanation. No defense.
Simply pray:
"Lord, I return to You here."
Then rest.

Prayer
Father,
I bring You my weakness without hiding.
I release the need to appear strong
and receive Your sufficient grace.
Teach me to return quickly
and to trust that You are forming me
even where I feel most fragile.
I depend on You.
Amen.

Declaration
Speak this aloud:
God's grace meets me in weakness.
Failure does not disqualify me from obedience.
I return quickly and honestly to God.
My life is being formed through grace, not perfection.
I rise again by God's strength.

Commitment to Obedience
Today, I commit to **grace-filled obedience**.
I will not hide my weakness
or abandon alignment when I fall.
I choose humility, return, and trust.

Closing Orientation
You are not finished.
You are being formed.
Tomorrow, we will explore **how obedience reshapes our identity—not as achievers, but as sons and daughters.**

DAY THIRTEEN
From Achievement to Identity

Why Obedience Flows From Who You Are

K EY FOCUS SCRIPTURES

- **Romans 8:15–16** — *You received the Spirit of adoption...*
- **John 1:12–13** — *To all who received Him... He gave the right to become children of God.*
- **Galatians 4:6–7** — *Because you are sons, God sent the Spirit of His Son into our hearts...*

Scripture Reading (Read Slowly)
"You did not receive a spirit that makes you a slave again to fear, but you received the Spirit of sonship."
— Romans 8:15
Notice what obedience is *not* rooted in: fear.

Devotional Reflection
One of the most exhausting distortions of obedience is when it is driven by achievement rather than identity.

When obedience is fueled by achievement, we strive to earn approval. We obey to prove sincerity, to validate faith, or to quiet insecurity. This kind of obedience is fragile. It depends on performance and collapses under failure.

Scripture presents a different foundation.

Obedience flows most naturally from **belonging**.

Before **C. S. Lewis** ever articulated Christian doctrine clearly, he had to unlearn a deeply ingrained assumption: that faith was something to be earned through correctness or effort. Christianity, he discovered, does not recruit achievers—it adopts children.

This changes everything.

Children do not obey to become family.

They obey because they already belong.

When identity precedes obedience, the posture shifts. We no longer obey to secure God's acceptance; we obey because we live within it. Fear loosens its grip. Performance loses its power. Obedience becomes response rather than requirement.

This does not make obedience optional.

It makes it relational.

Day 13 invites you to examine what has been driving your obedience.

If obedience has felt heavy, it may be because it has been powered by self-effort rather than sonship. If failure has produced shame rather than return, identity may still be anchored in performance.

God does not motivate obedience by threat.

He forms it through love.

When identity is settled, obedience becomes freer. We are no longer trying to earn a place—we are learning how to live from one.

Heart Examination

Sit with these questions quietly.

1. **What has most often motivated your obedience—fear, duty, gratitude, or belonging?**
2. **How do you respond internally when you fall short—do you question your worth or return as a child?**
3. **What would change if obedience flowed from identity rather than performance?**

Today's Practice (Identity-Forming)

Today's practice is **receiving**.

Find a quiet moment and speak this aloud slowly:

"I belong to God."

Repeat it three times.

Let it settle deeper each time.

Do not add explanation.

Just receive it.

Prayer

Father,

Thank You that You have not called me to earn Your love.

Thank You that I belong to You.

Heal the places where I have obeyed out of fear or performance.

Teach me obedience that flows from identity—

secure, loved, and free.

I receive my place as Your child.

Amen.

Declaration

Speak this aloud:

I am a child of God.

Obedience flows from belonging, not fear.

I do not strive for approval—I live from it.

My identity is secure in Christ.

I obey as one who is loved.

Commitment to Obedience

Today, I commit to **identity-rooted obedience**.

I release performance-driven faith

and receive my place as God's child.

I choose to live and obey from belonging.

Closing Orientation

Let today be gentle.

Identity settles slowly,

but once settled, it sustains obedience deeply.

Tomorrow, we will explore **how obedience reshapes our understanding of freedom—not as independence, but as alignment**.

DAY FOURTEEN
Freedom Through Alignment

Why Obedience Does Not Restrict You

KEY FOCUS SCRIPTURES

- **John 8:31–36** — *The truth will set you free.*
- **Romans 6:16–18** — *You have been set free from sin and have become slaves to righteousness.*
- **Psalm 119:45** — *I will walk about in freedom, for I have sought out Your precepts.*

Scripture Reading (Read Slowly)
"If the Son sets you free, you will be free indeed."
— John 8:36
Pause.
Notice **who** defines freedom.

Devotional Reflection
Modern culture often defines freedom as **self-direction**.

To be free, we are told, is to answer to no one, to follow our desires without interference, to remain unbound by authority. Yet Scripture offers a radically different vision. Freedom is not found in independence—it is found in **alignment**.

Before **C. S. Lewis** fully embraced Christianity, one of his greatest fears was that obedience would restrict him. He assumed surrender would narrow his life, limit his joy, and constrain his identity. What he discovered instead was the opposite: self-rule had not freed him—it had fragmented him.

Misalignment always produces strain.

A life disconnected from its true center must work harder to sustain itself. Desires pull in competing directions. Choices create conflict. Independence promises freedom but delivers restlessness.

Jesus exposes this illusion directly. Freedom, He teaches, does not come from removing authority, but from submitting to the right one. Truth does not confine us—it liberates us from what enslaves.

Day 14 invites you to examine what freedom has meant in your life.

Where obedience has felt restrictive, it may be because alignment has not yet been trusted. Where independence has felt freeing, it may be because its cost has not yet been counted.

Freedom is not the absence of limits.

It is the presence of purpose.

When obedience aligns us with God's design, resistance fades. Choices become clearer. Desire stabilizes. Peace emerges—not because effort has ceased, but because life is finally ordered around what is true.

This is the freedom Scripture promises.

Not the freedom to do anything,

but the freedom to become who you were made to be.

Heart Examination

Sit with these questions quietly.

1. **How have you typically defined freedom in your life?**
2. **Where has independence brought restlessness rather than peace?**
3. **What might alignment with God's truth make possible that self-direction cannot?**

Today's Practice (Reframing Freedom)

Today's practice is **redefinition**.

Choose **one area** where obedience has felt restrictive.

Pray this slowly:

"Lord, show me how alignment here leads to freedom."

Do not argue with the resistance.

Just ask for sight.

Prayer

Father,

I confess that I have often equated freedom with control.

Teach me to recognize freedom as alignment with truth.

Release me from the strain of self-rule

and lead me into the peace of obedience.

I trust Your design for my life.

Amen.

Declaration

Speak this aloud:

Freedom is found in alignment with God.

Obedience does not restrict me—it restores me.

I walk in truth, not independence.

My life is ordered around what is real.

I am free indeed.

Commitment to Obedience

Today, I commit to **trusting God's definition of freedom**.

I release the illusion that independence brings life

and choose alignment as the path to peace.

Closing Orientation

Let this day reset assumptions.

Freedom is not lost in obedience.

It is discovered there.

Tomorrow, we will explore **how obedience reshapes our relationship with time, patience, and waiting.**

DAY FIFTEEN
Learning God's Pace

Why Obedience Reshapes How We Wait

KEY FOCUS SCRIPTURES

- **Ecclesiastes 3:1** — *There is a time for everything...*
- **Isaiah 40:31** — *Those who wait on the Lord shall renew their strength.*
- **Psalm 27:14** — *Wait for the Lord; be strong, and let your heart take courage.*

Scripture Reading (Read Slowly)
"Those who wait on the Lord shall renew their strength."
— Isaiah 40:31
Pause.
Notice that waiting is not passive—it is relational.

Devotional Reflection
One of the most difficult adjustments obedience requires is a change in **pace.**

We are accustomed to urgency. We equate faithfulness with speed and assume that obedience should produce visible results quickly. When progress feels slow, we grow restless. When answers delay, we question alignment.

Scripture presents a different rhythm.

Before **C. S. Lewis** ever bore lasting fruit through his writing and witness, much of his obedience unfolded slowly—through waiting, patience, and unseen preparation. His formation did not follow urgency; it followed *timing.*

Waiting in Scripture is not inactivity.

It is **attentive trust.**

To wait on the Lord is not to pause life—it is to remain aligned while God works beyond our visibility. Waiting teaches us to release control over outcomes and to trust God's purposes even when clarity unfolds gradually.

This challenges us deeply.

We want obedience to accelerate progress.

God uses obedience to **stabilize** us.

Day 15 invites you to reconsider impatience—not as a personality trait, but as a spiritual posture. Where impatience dominates, trust is often strained. Where patience grows, obedience matures.

Waiting exposes what we depend on most.

If we rely on outcomes, waiting frustrates us.

If we rely on God, waiting strengthens us.

Obedience reshapes time by teaching us to remain faithful without demanding immediacy. It forms endurance—the quiet confidence that God's work does not require our pressure to be effective.

This is where strength is renewed.

Not through speed,

but through steady alignment.

Heart Examination

Sit with these questions quietly.

1. **Where do you feel most impatient in your spiritual life right now?**
2. **How do you typically respond when God's timing differs from your expectations?**
3. **What might God be forming in you through waiting that speed could not produce?**

Today's Practice (Patient Alignment)

Today's practice is **unhurried trust**.

Choose **one area** where you feel tempted to rush progress.

Pray this slowly:

"Lord, I trust Your timing here."

Do not revisit the issue today.

Let it rest.

Prayer

Father,

Teach me to wait without withdrawing

and to trust without controlling.

Renew my strength as I remain aligned with You.

Release me from urgency that strains my faith

and form patience that deepens obedience.

I rest in Your timing.

Amen.

Declaration

Speak this aloud:

I trust God's timing in my life.

Waiting does not weaken my obedience—it strengthens it.

I remain aligned without rushing outcomes.

God is working beyond what I can see.

My strength is renewed as I wait on the Lord.

Commitment to Obedience

Today, I commit to **patient obedience**.

I release the need to accelerate God's work

and choose steady alignment over urgency.

Closing Orientation

Let today slow you.

Waiting is not delay.

It is formation.

Tomorrow, we will explore **how obedience reshapes the way we handle power, influence, and responsibility.**

DAY SIXTEEN
Power Reordered by Obedience

Why Influence Is Formed Before It Is Entrusted

KEY FOCUS SCRIPTURES

- **Luke 22:25–27** — *The greatest among you should be like the youngest...*
- **Matthew 20:26–28** — *Whoever wants to become great among you must be your servant.*
- **1 Peter 5:2–3** — *Not lording it over those entrusted to you, but being examples...*

Scripture Reading (Read Slowly)
"I am among you as one who serves."
— Luke 22:27
Notice how Jesus defines authority.

Devotional Reflection
Few things test obedience like **influence**.

Power amplifies what already exists in the heart. If obedience has not reshaped our motives, influence will expose them. Scripture consistently reveals that God does not first ask *what* we can do—He forms *who* we are before entrusting responsibility.

Before **C. S. Lewis** carried public influence, his obedience had already been reordered around humility. When recognition came, it did not define him because obedience had already grounded him. His authority flowed from service, not self-importance.

This is countercultural.

We often pursue influence as validation. We assume responsibility confirms maturity. Yet Scripture reverses the order: maturity precedes responsibility. Obedience reshapes our understanding of power by teaching us to hold it lightly and steward it faithfully.

Power without obedience becomes control.

Power shaped by obedience becomes care.

Day 16 invites you to examine how you relate to influence—whether large or small. Leadership in Scripture is not about position; it is about posture. Authority is not about being noticed; it is about being trustworthy.

Obedience trains us to lead without grasping, to serve without performing, and to carry responsibility without entitlement. It removes the need to be seen and replaces it with the desire to be faithful.

This is how God protects both us and those we serve.

Heart Examination

Sit with these questions quietly.

1. **How do you typically respond to responsibility or influence?**
2. **What motives surface when you are given authority—control, fear, service, or humility?**
3. **Where might God be forming your character before expanding your influence?**

Today's Practice (Servant Alignment)

Today's practice is **quiet service**.

Choose **one responsibility** you carry—at work, home, church, or community.

Fulfill it today **without asserting control or seeking recognition**.

Serve attentively.

Release the need to be noticed.

PRAYER

Father,

Teach me to carry responsibility with humility.

Form my heart before expanding my influence.

Guard me from using power to control
and shape me to serve with faithfulness.
I trust You to entrust what I am ready to steward.
Amen.

Declaration

Speak this aloud:
God forms my character before my influence.
I lead through service, not control.
Obedience reshapes how I carry responsibility.
I steward authority with humility and care.
I serve as Christ served.

Commitment to Obedience

Today, I commit to **obedient stewardship**.
I release the need for recognition
and choose faithfulness in responsibility.

Closing Orientation

Let today steady you.
Influence grows safest
when obedience leads the way.

Tomorrow, we will explore **how obedience reshapes our relationship with truth—not as information, but as formation**.

DAY SEVENTEEN
When Truth Demands Obedience

Why Knowing Is Not the Same as Being Formed

KEY FOCUS SCRIPTURES

- **John 17:17** — *Sanctify them by the truth; Your word is truth.*
- **James 1:22–25** — *Do not merely listen to the word, and so deceive yourselves.*
- **2 Timothy 3:16–17** — *All Scripture is God-breathed and useful...*

Scripture Reading (Read Slowly)
"Do not merely listen to the word, and so deceive yourselves.
Do what it says."
— James 1:22
Pause.
Notice that self-deception does not come from ignorance—but from distance between knowing and doing.

Devotional Reflection
One of the most subtle obstacles to obedience is **familiarity with truth**.

We live in an age saturated with information. Sermons are accessible. Scripture is searchable. Insight is abundant. Yet Scripture warns that knowing truth without obedience can deceive us into thinking formation is happening when it is not.

Truth, in Scripture, is never neutral.

It either shapes us—or exposes us.

Before **C. S. Lewis** became known for explaining Christianity clearly, he wrestled with a dangerous temptation: to treat truth as something to analyze rather than something to obey. His intellectual rigor could have become a refuge from surrender. Instead, truth confronted him.

This is why Mere Christianity remains unsettling.

It does not allow readers to remain observers. It insists that truth makes claims on the will, not just the mind. Lewis understood that Christianity does not ask us to *agree*—it asks us to *yield*.

We often assume that truth will automatically change us once understood. Scripture disagrees. Transformation requires response. Truth must be welcomed, practiced, and embodied to do its work.

Day 17 invites you to examine how truth functions in your life.

Where truth is admired but not practiced, formation stalls.

Where truth is obeyed, even imperfectly, formation deepens.

Obedience is not an add-on to truth.

It is truth's intended destination.

God does not reveal truth to impress us.

He reveals it to remake us.

Heart Examination

Sit with these questions quietly.

1. **Where has truth become familiar but not formative in your life?**
2. **What truths do you understand clearly but struggle to obey consistently?**
3. **How might obedience deepen your relationship with truth rather than limit it?**

Today's Practice (Truth-in-Action)

Today's practice is **embodied truth**.

Identify **one truth** you already know well—about forgiveness, humility, patience, honesty, or love.

Practice it **once today in a concrete way**.

Let truth move from concept to action.

Prayer

Father,

Deliver me from knowing truth without living it.

Let Your Word shape my choices, not just my thoughts.

Teach me to welcome truth as a forming power,
not merely an idea to admire.
I submit myself to what You reveal.
Amen.

Declaration

Speak this aloud:
God's truth forms my life.
I do not merely hear—I obey.
Truth reshapes my actions and desires.
I submit my will to what is revealed.
I am being sanctified by truth.

Commitment to Obedience

Today, I commit to **truth-shaped obedience**.
I will not separate understanding from action.
I choose to live what I know.

Closing Orientation

Truth is not complete until it is lived.

Tomorrow, we will explore **how obedience reshapes our relationship with suffering—not as punishment, but as participation.**

DAY EIGHTEEN
When Obedience Meets Suffering

Why Pain Can Become a Place of Participation

KEY FOCUS SCRIPTURES

- **1 Peter 4:12–13** — *Rejoice insofar as you share Christ's sufferings...*
- **Romans 8:17–18** — *We share in His sufferings in order that we may also share in His glory.*
- **2 Corinthians 4:16–17** — *These light and momentary troubles are achieving for us an eternal glory...*

Scripture Reading (Read Slowly)
"Do not be surprised at the fiery ordeal that has come on you to test you."
— 1 Peter 4:12
Notice the word **participation**, not punishment.

Devotional Reflection

Few things unsettle obedience like suffering.

When pain enters our lives, we instinctively ask *why*. We search for explanations, causes, or mistakes. We assume suffering must mean something has gone wrong—either with us or with God. Scripture offers a more sobering and hopeful truth: suffering is not always a detour from obedience; sometimes it is the **terrain** obedience must walk through.

Before **C. S. Lewis** spoke openly about Christian suffering, he lived it. He did not romanticize pain or minimize its cost. Lewis acknowledged suffering as one of the deepest challenges to belief—and yet, he came to see it as a place where obedience becomes profoundly real.

Suffering reveals what obedience rests on.

If obedience is transactional, suffering feels unfair.

If obedience is relational, suffering becomes a place of trust.

Scripture does not promise exemption from pain. It promises presence within it. To share in Christ's sufferings is not to seek pain, but to remain aligned with God even when obedience leads through loss, misunderstanding, or endurance.

This reframes suffering entirely.

Suffering is not evidence of abandonment.

It is often evidence of proximity.

Day 18 invites you to consider how you respond when obedience becomes costly. Do you retreat? Do you negotiate? Or do you remain present, trusting that God is at work even where clarity is absent?

Suffering strips obedience of illusion. It removes performance and exposes motive. What remains is either resentment—or surrender.

Christ chose obedience even unto suffering, not because pain was good, but because love was greater. And in following Him, we are invited into that same posture—not as victims, but as participants.

Heart Examination

Sit with these questions quietly.

1. How do you typically interpret suffering in your spiritual life?
2. Where has pain challenged your trust or obedience recently?
3. What might it mean to remain aligned with God even without answers?

Today's Practice (Presence in Pain)

Today's practice is **staying present**.

Identify **one area of discomfort, grief, or difficulty** you would normally avoid or rush past.

Do not solve it today.

Do not spiritualize it.

Simply pray:

"Lord, I remain with You here."

Stay present for a few quiet moments.

Prayer

Father,

I do not understand all my suffering,

but I trust that You are present within it.

Teach me obedience that does not retreat

when pain arises.

Help me remain aligned with You

even when clarity is delayed.

I share my weakness with You.

Amen.

Declaration

Speak this aloud:

Suffering does not separate me from God.

I remain aligned even in difficulty.

Obedience holds steady through pain.

I participate in Christ's life and trust His work.

God is present with me here.

Commitment to Obedience

Today, I commit to **obedience that remains present**.

I will not abandon alignment

when suffering challenges my understanding.

I trust God's presence in every season.

CLOSING ORIENTATION

Do not rush past today.
Suffering forms depth
that comfort cannot.

Tomorrow, we will explore **how obedience reshapes our understanding of hope—not as optimism, but as endurance.**

DAY NINETEEN
Hope That Endures

Why Christian Hope Is Stronger Than Optimism

KEY FOCUS SCRIPTURES

- **Romans 5:3–5** — *Suffering produces perseverance; perseverance, character; and character, hope.*
- **Hebrews 6:19** — *We have this hope as an anchor for the soul, firm and secure.*
- **Lamentations 3:31–33** — *Though He brings grief, He will show compassion...*

Scripture Reading (Read Slowly)
"We have this hope as an anchor for the soul, firm and secure."
— Hebrews 6:19
Notice what hope does.
It anchors—it does not float.

Devotional Reflection
Hope is often misunderstood.

We confuse hope with positivity, with expecting things to improve, with believing that circumstances will resolve favorably. Scripture offers a more resilient vision. Christian hope is not tied to outcomes—it is anchored in **God's faithfulness**, regardless of outcome.

This distinction matters deeply.

Optimism rises and falls with circumstances.

Hope remains when circumstances do not change.

Before **C. S. Lewis** wrote about hope with clarity, he learned its cost. Lewis did not deny suffering or minimize grief. He rejected shallow reassurance. What he came to trust instead was a hope rooted not in comfort, but in truth—a hope that could endure disappointment without collapsing.

Hope, in Scripture, is forged.

It is formed through perseverance.

It is strengthened through endurance.

It matures through waiting.

Day 19 invites you to examine what your hope has been resting on.

If hope depends on relief, it will waver.

If hope depends on God's character, it will hold.

This does not mean pretending pain does not exist. Biblical hope looks suffering in the face and refuses to let it define reality. It anchors the soul in something deeper than experience—something unchanging.

Obedience and hope grow together.

As obedience trains us to remain aligned without immediate reward, hope learns to rest without immediate resolution. Together, they form endurance—the quiet strength to continue faithfully even when clarity delays.

This is not passive hope.

It is resilient trust.

Heart Examination

Sit with these questions quietly.

1. **What has your hope been tied to most strongly—outcomes or God's character?**
2. **How do you respond internally when things do not improve as expected?**
3. **What might it mean to anchor your hope somewhere deeper than circumstances?**

Today's Practice (Anchoring Hope)

Today's practice is **anchored remembrance**.

Write down or quietly recall **one truth about God** that remains unchanged regardless of your situation (His faithfulness, presence, mercy, sovereignty).

Repeat it slowly throughout the day.

Let hope rest there.

Prayer

Father,

Teach me hope that endures,

not hope that depends on relief.

Anchor my soul in Your character

when circumstances remain unresolved.

Help me trust You steadily,

even when outcomes are unclear.

You are my secure foundation.

Amen.

Declaration

Speak this aloud:

My hope is anchored in God.

Circumstances do not define my faith.

I endure with confidence in truth.

God's faithfulness remains unshaken.

My soul is firm and secure.

Commitment to Obedience

Today, I commit to **anchored hope**.

I will not measure God's faithfulness

by immediate outcomes.

I trust His character and remain aligned.

Closing Orientation

Hope matures quietly.

It does not rush resolution—

it steadies the soul.

Tomorrow, we will explore **how obedience reshapes our understanding of love—not as emotion, but as disciplined commitment.**

DAY TWENTY
Love That Learns to Stay

Why Obedience Trains the Heart to Love Well

KEY FOCUS SCRIPTURES

- **John 14:15** — *If you love Me, you will keep My commandments.*
- **1 Corinthians 13:4–7** — *Love is patient, love is kind...*
- **1 John 5:3** — *This is love for God: to keep His commands.*

Scripture Reading (Read Slowly)
"This is love for God: to keep His commands.
And His commands are not burdensome."
— 1 John 5:3
Pause.
Notice how Scripture defines love.

Devotional Reflection
Modern culture treats love as an emotion—something felt, followed, and withdrawn when it fades.

Scripture treats love as a **commitment**—something practiced, sustained, and proven through faithfulness. This difference matters deeply. When love is reduced to feeling, it becomes unstable. When love is formed through obedience, it becomes resilient.

Before **C. S. Lewis** wrote about Christian love with clarity, he learned that love must be trained. Affection fluctuates. Desire shifts. Emotion rises and falls. Obedience teaches love to stay when feeling alone cannot carry it.

This is why Scripture links love so closely with obedience.

Love is not merely expressed—it is enacted.

It is patient when irritated.

Kind when inconvenient.

Faithful when unseen.

Day 20 invites you to examine how you understand love.

If love depends on emotion, obedience feels optional.

If love is commitment, obedience becomes natural.

Christian love is not cold or mechanical. It is disciplined warmth—formed through repeated choices to remain aligned with God and faithful to others, even when feeling lags behind intention.

This kind of love grows slowly.

Obedience trains us to act lovingly before we feel loving. Over time, feeling follows formation. The heart learns to love what the will consistently chooses.

This is how love matures.

Not by intensity,

but by endurance.

Heart Examination

Sit with these questions quietly.

1. **How have you typically defined love—emotion or commitment?**
2. **Where has obedience challenged your understanding of love?**
3. **What relationship or responsibility requires disciplined love right now?**

Today's Practice (Committed Love)

Today's practice is **intentional faithfulness**.

Choose **one relationship or responsibility** where love feels ordinary, strained, or unnoticed.

Express love today through **action**, not feeling:

- A kind word
- A patient response
- A faithful follow-through

Do not wait to feel loving.

Choose to be loving.

Prayer

Father,

Teach me love that endures,

not love that depends on emotion.

Form my heart through obedient faithfulness

so that love becomes steady and true.

Help me remain committed

when feelings fluctuate.

I choose love shaped by obedience.

Amen.

Declaration

Speak this aloud:

Love is formed through obedience.

I love with commitment, not impulse.

God's commands train my heart to love well.

I remain faithful even when feeling fades.

My love grows stronger through alignment.

Commitment to Obedience

Today, I commit to **disciplined love**.

I choose faithfulness over fluctuation

and obedience over emotion.

Closing Orientation

You have reached a hinge in the journey.

From here forward, obedience moves

from formation into **mission**.

Tomorrow, we will explore **how obedience reshapes our sense of purpose—not as self-fulfillment, but as faithful calling**.

DAY TWENTY-ONE
Purpose Formed by Obedience

Why Calling Is Discovered Through Faithfulness

KEY FOCUS SCRIPTURES

- **Ephesians 2:10** — *Created in Christ Jesus for good works...*
- **Luke 16:10–12** — *Faithful in little, faithful in much.*
- **1 Corinthians 7:17** — *Each should live as the Lord has assigned...*

Scripture Reading (Read Slowly)
"We are God's workmanship,
created in Christ Jesus to do good works,
which God prepared in advance for us to do."
— Ephesians 2:10
Pause.
Notice that purpose is **prepared**, not improvised.

Devotional Reflection

Purpose is often treated as something to be discovered suddenly—through clarity, passion, or opportunity.

Scripture presents a quieter reality: purpose is revealed **through faithfulness**. Calling does not usually arrive as a dramatic announcement. It unfolds as obedience practiced consistently in ordinary places.

Before **C. S. Lewis** understood the reach his work would have, his obedience focused on what was immediately in front of him—teaching, writing faithfully, telling the truth carefully. Purpose followed faithfulness. It did not precede it.

This matters.

When we chase purpose without obedience, we often chase visibility. We look for roles rather than readiness, platforms rather than posture. Scripture redirects us: God entrusts greater responsibility to those who are faithful where they are.

Purpose is not found by asking, *"What am I meant to do?"*

It is formed by asking, *"How can I be faithful here?"*

Day 21 invites you to release pressure.

You do not need full clarity to be obedient.

You need willingness where you stand.

Calling is not a detour from obedience; it is obedience extended over time. Faithfulness in small things trains the heart to carry greater ones without distortion.

God's purposes are not fragile.

They do not require you to rush ahead of formation.

They emerge naturally where obedience remains steady.

Heart Examination

Sit with these questions quietly.

1. **Where have you been tempted to chase purpose rather than practice faithfulness?**
2. **What responsibilities are already in front of you right now?**
3. **How might obedience here be shaping future calling?**

Today's Practice (Faithful Presence)

Today's practice is **attentive faithfulness.**

Identify **one responsibility or opportunity** already entrusted to you—work, family, service, study, or care.

Give it **your full attention today.**

Do not rush through it.

Do not minimize it.

Treat it as purpose in formation.

PRAYER

Father,

139

Teach me to trust that You reveal purpose through obedience.
Release me from anxiety about the future
and anchor me in faithfulness today.
Help me serve well where I am
and trust You with what comes next.
I offer You my present alignment.
Amen.

Declaration

Speak this aloud:
God's purpose unfolds through my obedience.
I am faithful where I am.
Small acts of obedience shape lasting calling.
I trust God with my future and align today.
My life is being formed for good works.

Commitment to Obedience

Today, I commit to **faithful presence**.
I release the need for premature clarity
and choose obedience in what is already entrusted to me.

Closing Orientation

Purpose grows quietly.
Faithfulness prepares the way.
Tomorrow, we will explore **how obedience reshapes ambition—not by removing it, but by purifying it**.

DAY TWENTY-TWO
Ambition Reordered

When Obedience Purifies What Drives You

K EY FOCUS SCRIPTURES

- **Matthew 6:33** — *Seek first the kingdom of God...*
- **James 3:13–17** — *Wisdom from above is pure, peaceable, gentle...*
- **Philippians 2:3–5** — *Do nothing out of selfish ambition...*

Scripture Reading (Read Slowly)
"Do nothing out of selfish ambition or vain conceit.
Rather, in humility value others above yourselves."
— Philippians 2:3
Pause.
Notice that Scripture does not erase ambition—it **qualifies** it.

Devotional Reflection
Ambition is not the enemy of obedience.
Unexamined ambition is.
Many believers assume that following Christ requires abandoning desire, drive, or aspiration. Scripture offers a more discerning path. God does not remove ambition—He **reorders it**.

Before **C. S. Lewis** learned to steward influence faithfully, ambition had to be purified. The desire to be right, to be heard, to be recognized—these impulses were not erased by faith. They were refined. Obedience redirected what ambition was *for*.

Ambition answers the question: *What am I moving toward?*
When ambition is self-centered, obedience feels restrictive.

When ambition is God-centered, obedience becomes clarifying.

Scripture distinguishes between selfish ambition and holy aspiration. One seeks recognition; the other seeks faithfulness. One pursues visibility; the other pursues alignment. One elevates self; the other advances God's purposes.

Day 22 invites you to examine what drives you beneath the surface.

Ambition left unchecked becomes comparison.

Ambition purified becomes service.

Obedience does not flatten desire. It gives desire a new center. It teaches us to seek the Kingdom first—not as an abstract idea, but as a lived priority that reshapes goals, choices, and expectations.

When ambition is aligned, striving gives way to steadiness. We are no longer driven by anxiety to prove ourselves. We are moved by trust to serve faithfully.

This is ambition healed.

Heart Examination

Sit with these questions quietly.

1. **What ambitions currently motivate your decisions?**
2. **Where might desire for recognition or success be shaping your obedience?**
3. **What would it look like to seek God's Kingdom first in your aspirations?**

Today's Practice (Purified Intention)

Today's practice is **intentional alignment**.

Choose **one goal or ambition** you are actively pursuing.

Pray this honestly:

"Lord, reorder this ambition toward Your purposes."

Then take **one small step** today that reflects humility, service, or faithfulness rather than visibility.

Prayer

Father,

You know the desires that drive me.

Purify my ambition and align it with Your Kingdom.

Remove what is rooted in fear or pride

and strengthen what serves Your purposes.

Teach me to seek You first in all I pursue.

Amen.

Declaration

Speak this aloud:

My ambition is aligned with God's Kingdom.

Obedience purifies what drives me.

I seek faithfulness over recognition.

My desires are being reordered by truth.

I move steadily toward God's purposes.

Commitment to Obedience

Today, I commit to **Kingdom-centered ambition.**

I release self-centered striving

and choose obedience that aligns my desires with God's will.

Closing Orientation

Ambition does not disappear.

It is **redirected**.

Tomorrow, we will explore **how obedience reshapes success—not by redefining achievement, but by measuring fruit.**

DAY TWENTY-THREE

Success Measured by Fruit

Why Obedience Redefines What It Means to Succeed

K EY FOCUS SCRIPTURES

- **John 15:4–8** — *Remain in Me, and you will bear much fruit.*
- **Matthew 7:16–20** — *By their fruit you will recognize them.*
- **Galatians 5:22–23** — *The fruit of the Spirit is...*

Scripture Reading (Read Slowly)
"By their fruit you will recognize them."
— Matthew 7:16
Pause.
Notice that Scripture evaluates lives by **outcome**, not image.

Devotional Reflection
Success is one of the most quietly dangerous concepts in modern faith.

We often measure success by visibility, growth, affirmation, or productivity. Even in spiritual contexts, we can confuse momentum with maturity and activity with alignment. Scripture offers a different measure entirely: **fruit**.

Fruit is not manufactured.

It is produced.

Before **C. S. Lewis** became widely influential, the fruit of his obedience was already visible—clarity of thought, humility in conviction, patience in dialogue, faithfulness in discipline. Public recognition came later. Fruit came first.

This order matters.

Fruit cannot be rushed.

It cannot be faked.

It cannot be sustained without alignment.

Obedience reshapes success by shifting focus from outcomes we control to fruit God produces. It asks not, *"What have I achieved?"* but *"What is being formed?"* Love, patience, self-control, faithfulness—these are not flashy metrics, but they are unmistakable.

Day 23 invites you to examine how you evaluate your life.

Where success is measured by results alone, pressure increases.

Where success is measured by fruit, peace grows.

Jesus does not ask for impressive output.

He invites abiding.

Fruit emerges naturally where obedience remains rooted. Over time, the fruit becomes visible—not always to us first, but unmistakably to others. This is why Scripture says we are "recognized" by fruit. It reveals what kind of tree we are becoming.

Success, in God's Kingdom, is not about how far you have gone.

It is about what is growing where you stand.

Heart Examination

Sit with these questions quietly.

1. **How have you typically measured success in your life?**
2. **What kind of fruit is currently evident in you—patience, love, peace, self-control?**
3. **What fruit might God be growing that you have overlooked because it feels ordinary?**

Today's Practice (Fruit Awareness)

Today's practice is **noticing fruit.**

Throughout the day, pay attention to moments where:

- You respond with patience instead of irritation
- You choose restraint instead of impulse
- You act with kindness without recognition

At the end of the day, thank God for **one small piece of fruit** you noticed.

Prayer

Father,

Teach me to value fruit over recognition.

Help me remain rooted in You

so that what grows in my life reflects Your Spirit.

Release me from false measures of success

and anchor me in what You are forming.

I choose to abide.

Amen.

Declaration

Speak this aloud:

I measure success by fruit, not visibility.

God produces growth through obedience.

I remain rooted and aligned.

What God is forming in me matters.

My life bears lasting fruit.

Commitment to Obedience

Today, I commit to **fruit-bearing obedience**.

I release false measures of success

and trust God to produce what endures.

Closing Orientation

Fruit grows quietly.

Tomorrow, we will explore **how obedience reshapes our understanding of legacy—not as memory, but as multiplication.**

DAY TWENTY-FOUR
Legacy That Multiplies

Why Obedience Outlives Visibility

KEY FOCUS SCRIPTURES

- **2 Timothy 2:2** — *Entrust to faithful people who will be able to teach others also.*
- **Psalm 145:4** — *One generation commends Your works to another.*
- **John 12:24** — *Unless a grain of wheat falls into the earth and dies... it bears much fruit.*

Scripture Reading (Read Slowly)
"Unless a grain of wheat falls into the earth and dies,
it remains alone; but if it dies, it bears much fruit."
— John 12:24
Pause.
Notice that fruit requires **release**, not preservation.

Devotional Reflection
Legacy is often misunderstood as what remains *about* us after we are gone.

Scripture defines legacy as what continues *through* others because we were faithful. Legacy is not memory—it is multiplication. It is not how long we are remembered; it is how deeply obedience reproduces life beyond us.

Before **C. S. Lewis** could ever imagine the reach of his work, he focused on faithfulness rather than impact. He wrote, taught, and spoke with clarity because obedience demanded truthfulness—not because legacy was guaranteed. The multiplication came later, beyond his control.

This is the Kingdom pattern.

Seeds do not announce their future harvest.

They simply fall into the ground and obey their design.

Day 24 invites you to release the pressure to secure your own legacy. Obedience that clings to visibility cannot multiply. Obedience that releases control creates space for God to produce fruit far beyond our lifetime.

Legacy grows where obedience is transferable—where truth is lived, shared, and entrusted to others who will carry it forward. This is why Scripture emphasizes faithfulness to people, not platforms.

You do not need to know who will be affected by your obedience.

You need to remain faithful where you are.

God handles multiplication.

Legacy is not built by self-preservation.

It is formed by surrender.

Heart Examination

Sit with these questions quietly.

1. **How have you thought about legacy—reputation or reproduction?**
2. **Where might God be asking you to release control rather than preserve influence?**
3. **Who could be quietly shaped by your obedience right now?**

Today's Practice (Entrusting Faithfully)

Today's practice is **intentional investment**.

Encourage, support, or speak truth to **one person**—without agenda or expectation of return.

Do it simply.

Do it faithfully.

Let God handle the fruit.

Prayer

Father,

Release me from the need to secure my own legacy.

Teach me to trust You with multiplication.

Help me invest faithfully in others

and surrender control over outcomes.

Let my obedience bear fruit beyond what I can see.

Amen.

Declaration

Speak this aloud:

My obedience multiplies beyond my visibility.

God produces fruit through faithful surrender.

I release control and trust God with legacy.

What I invest in others endures.

My life bears fruit beyond me.

Commitment to Obedience

Today, I commit to **legacy-minded obedience.**

I will invest faithfully

and trust God to multiply what I release.

Closing Orientation

Legacy is forming quietly.

Tomorrow, we will explore **how obedience reshapes our understanding of death and mortality—not as loss, but as completion.**

DAY TWENTY-FIVE
Obedience at the Edge of Mortality

Why Death Completes What Obedience Begins

KEY FOCUS SCRIPTURES

- **Philippians 1:21–23** — *To live is Christ, and to die is gain.*
- **Hebrews 11:13–16** — *They were longing for a better country...*
- **2 Timothy 4:7–8** — *I have fought the good fight...*

Scripture Reading (Read Slowly)
"I have fought the good fight,
I have finished the race,
I have kept the faith."
— 2 Timothy 4:7
Pause.
Notice that Paul speaks of **completion**, not regret.

Devotional Reflection
Modern culture avoids death by denying it.

We distract ourselves with productivity, entertainment, and legacy-building, hoping not to face the reality that every life moves toward an ending. Scripture does not avoid death. It reframes it. Death is not the negation of obedience—it is its **culmination**.

For those who walk in alignment with God, death is not interruption. It is arrival.

Before **C. S. Lewis** reflected deeply on mortality, he wrestled with its implications. Death unsettles us because it exposes where our hope truly rests.

If obedience is rooted in outcomes, death feels like loss. If obedience is rooted in faithfulness, death feels like completion.

Scripture speaks of finishing well.

Not achieving everything.

Not avoiding all pain.

But remaining aligned until the end.

Day 25 invites you to examine how mortality shapes your obedience.

If death is feared, obedience often becomes anxious.

If death is accepted, obedience becomes focused.

Awareness of mortality clarifies priorities. It strips away trivial ambition and exposes what truly matters. Obedience becomes less about accumulation and more about faithfulness. Less about proving significance and more about living in alignment with God's purposes.

Death does not diminish a faithful life.

It seals it.

The Christian hope is not that we avoid death, but that death cannot undo what obedience has formed. What God begins in us, He completes—even beyond our final breath.

Heart Examination

Sit with these questions quietly.

1. **How does awareness of mortality influence your priorities?**
2. **What would "finishing well" look like in your life?**
3. **Where might obedience help you live more intentionally today?**

Today's Practice (Living with the End in View)

Today's practice is **intentional alignment**.

Choose **one activity or decision** today and ask:

"Would this matter if I were nearing the end of my life?"

Let that question refine your choice.

Prayer

Father,

Teach me to live with eternity in view.

Help me prioritize faithfulness over accumulation

and alignment over anxiety.

I trust that You complete what You begin
and that my obedience matters beyond this life.
I offer You my days.
Amen.

Declaration

Speak this aloud:
My life is oriented toward eternity.
Obedience prepares me to finish well.
Death does not undo God's work in me.
I live faithfully with the end in view.
My hope is secure in Christ.

Commitment to Obedience

Today, I commit to **eternal-minded obedience**.
I release fear of mortality
and choose alignment that endures beyond my lifetime.

Closing Orientation

Mortality clarifies obedience.

Tomorrow, we will explore **how obedience reshapes our understanding of resurrection—not as doctrine alone, but as daily hope.**

DAY TWENTY-SIX
Living the Resurrection Now

Why Obedience Is Shaped by What Is Yet to Come

KEY FOCUS SCRIPTURES

- **Romans 6:4–5** — *Just as Christ was raised from the dead... we too may live a new life.*
- **1 Corinthians 15:19–22** — *If only for this life we have hope in Christ...*
- **Colossians 3:1–4** — *Set your hearts on things above...*

Scripture Reading (Read Slowly)
"Just as Christ was raised from the dead through the glory of the Father, we too may live a new life."
— Romans 6:4
Notice the tense.
Resurrection shapes **how we live now.**

Devotional Reflection
Resurrection is often treated as future hope only—something we affirm doctrinally while living practically unchanged.

Scripture refuses that separation.

The resurrection of Christ is not merely an event to be remembered. It is a **reality to be embodied.** It declares that death does not have final authority, that failure does not have final say, and that obedience is not wasted—even when it costs everything.

Before **C. S. Lewis** spoke about resurrection with confidence, he learned to let future hope reshape present choices. Resurrection reframes obedience

153

because it assures us that what we surrender is not lost, and what we invest in Christ is not erased.

This changes the calculus of obedience.

If resurrection is true, obedience is never futile.

If resurrection is real, sacrifice is never final.

If resurrection is certain, faithfulness is always worthwhile.

Day 26 invites you to live forward.

Obedience grounded in resurrection is not anxious. It is steady. It does not cling tightly to comfort or control because it trusts that God restores what is laid down. Resurrection hope loosens our grip on self-preservation and strengthens our resolve to live truthfully now.

This is why Scripture urges us to "set our minds on things above." Not to escape the present—but to **interpret it correctly**. Resurrection teaches us that today is not the whole story. What seems lost may yet be raised. What feels small may yet be glorified.

Obedience becomes courageous when resurrection anchors it.

Heart Examination

Sit with these questions quietly.

1. **How does belief in resurrection shape your daily decisions—if at all?**
2. **What fears might loosen if you trusted that God restores what is surrendered?**
3. **Where is God inviting you to live with future hope shaping present obedience?**

Today's Practice (Resurrection-Oriented Choice)

Today's practice is **forward-looking obedience**.

Choose **one decision** today that feels costly, inconvenient, or unseen.

Make it anyway—

not because it feels good,

but because resurrection assures it matters.

Prayer

Father,

Anchor my obedience in resurrection hope.

Teach me to live today
in light of what You promise tomorrow.
Release my fear of loss
and strengthen my trust that You restore all things.
I live as one raised with Christ.
Amen.

Declaration

Speak this aloud:
I live in the power of Christ's resurrection.
Obedience is never wasted.
What I surrender, God restores.
My life is shaped by eternal hope.
I walk forward in confidence and faith.

Commitment to Obedience

Today, I commit to **resurrection-shaped obedience**.
I release fear of loss
and live faithfully in light of what God will complete.

Closing Orientation

Resurrection changes everything.

Tomorrow, we will explore **how obedience reshapes our relationship with judgment—not as fear, but as accountability rooted in hope.**

DAY TWENTY-SEVEN
Judgment Without Fear

Why Obedience Faces Accountability With Confidence

KEY FOCUS SCRIPTURES

- **2 Corinthians 5:10** — *We must all appear before the judgment seat of Christ.*
- **Romans 14:10–12** — *Each of us will give an account of ourselves to God.*
- **1 John 4:17–18** — *Perfect love drives out fear...*

Scripture Reading (Read Slowly)

"This is how love is made complete among us so that we will have confidence on the day of judgment."

— 1 John 4:17

Pause.

Notice the word **confidence**, not dread.

Devotional Reflection

Judgment is one of the most misunderstood themes in Christian faith.

Many believers quietly fear it. Others avoid it entirely. We imagine judgment as exposure without mercy, evaluation without grace, accounting without relationship. Scripture offers a different picture: judgment is not the enemy of obedience—it is its **clarifier**.

Judgment reveals what obedience has already been forming.

Before **C. S. Lewis** came to speak honestly about accountability, he wrestled with the idea that God's judgment would be arbitrary or crushing.

156

What he discovered instead was that judgment, rightly understood, is the unveiling of reality. It shows what has been shaped, what has endured, and what was aligned with truth.

Judgment is not about comparison.

It is about correspondence.

It reveals whether our lives have corresponded to the truth we professed. This is why Scripture connects judgment with love. Where obedience flows from love, fear loosens its grip. Where obedience has been sincere—even imperfect—judgment becomes confirmation rather than condemnation.

Fear thrives where obedience is performative.

Confidence grows where obedience is honest.

Day 27 invites you to examine how you relate to accountability.

If judgment feels terrifying, it may be because obedience has been driven by fear or image. If judgment feels clarifying, it is because obedience has been rooted in alignment rather than performance.

God does not judge to shame.

He judges to reveal.

Judgment completes formation by naming what was true. It affirms what obedience has quietly formed over time. For those who walk in Christ, judgment is not a threat—it is a testimony.

Heart Examination

Sit with these questions quietly.

1. **What emotions surface when you think about accountability before God?**
2. **Where might fear of judgment be revealing performance-driven obedience?**
3. **How could love-rooted obedience reshape your confidence before God?**

Today's Practice (Honest Alignment)

Today's practice is **truthful review**.

At the end of the day, ask yourself quietly:

"Where did my life align with truth today?"

Thank God for what was genuine.

Release what was not.

No shame.

Just honesty.

Prayer

Father,

Thank You that Your judgment is rooted in truth and love.

Remove fear where I have misunderstood accountability.

Teach me obedience that does not hide

and faithfulness that stands in the light.

I trust You to complete what You are forming in me.

Amen.

Declaration

Speak this aloud:

I face accountability with confidence in Christ.

Obedience aligns my life with truth.

God's judgment reveals what is real, not what is feared.

Love drives out fear in my obedience.

I live honestly before God.

Commitment to Obedience

Today, I commit to **transparent obedience**.

I will not hide from accountability

or perform for approval.

I choose alignment rooted in love and truth.

Closing Orientation

Judgment clarifies what obedience has shaped.

Tomorrow, we will explore **how obedience reshapes our understanding of reward—not as payment, but as participation in God's joy.**

DAY TWENTY-EIGHT

LIVING AS CHRIST'S AMBASSADOR EVERY DAY

K EY FOCUS SCRIPTURES
" Reward Without Transaction
Why Obedience Leads to Joy, Not Wages
Key Focus Scriptures

- **Matthew 25:21** — *Well done, good and faithful servant... enter into the joy of your master.*
- **Hebrews 11:6** — *He rewards those who earnestly seek Him.*
- **Psalm 16:11** — *In Your presence there is fullness of joy.*

Scripture Reading (Read Slowly)
"Well done, good and faithful servant...
enter into the joy of your master."
— Matthew 25:21
Pause.
Notice that the reward is **joy**, not compensation.
Devotional Reflection
Reward is often misunderstood as payment.

We instinctively treat obedience like labor and reward like wages—if we do enough, God owes us something. Scripture dismantles this framework gently but firmly. God does not reward obedience because He is obligated. He rewards obedience by **sharing His joy**.

The reward is relational.

Before **C. S. Lewis** came to understand Christian reward rightly, he struggled with the idea that reward diminished virtue. He assumed that true goodness should be disinterested—that reward would cheapen obedience. What he discovered instead was transformative: God's rewards are not external prizes; they are the natural fulfillment of alignment.

Reward completes obedience by drawing us deeper into God Himself.

When obedience is transactional, joy is fragile.

When obedience is relational, joy is inevitable.

Scripture consistently points to joy as the fruit of faithfulness. Not excitement. Not pleasure. Joy—steady, durable, shared. Obedience does not earn God's love; it positions us to **experience it more fully**.

Day 28 invites you to examine how you think about reward.

If you obey expecting return, disappointment often follows.

If you obey to remain aligned, joy quietly grows.

God does not stand at the end of obedience with a ledger.

He stands with open arms, inviting us further in.

The joy of obedience is not delayed gratification.

It is deeper participation.

Heart Examination

Sit with these questions quietly.

1. **How have you unconsciously treated obedience—as duty or relationship?**
2. **Where might you expect God to "pay you back" for faithfulness?**
3. **What would it look like to obey simply to remain close to God?**

Today's Practice (Joy-Oriented Obedience)

Today's practice is **relational obedience**.

Choose **one act of obedience** today—prayer, service, restraint, generosity. Before doing it, pray:

"Lord, I do this to remain close to You."

Afterward, pause briefly and notice any quiet joy or peace.

PRAYER

Father,

Release me from transactional faith.

Teach me obedience that delights in Your presence.

Let joy, not obligation, shape my faithfulness.

I receive reward as relationship,

not payment.

I enter Your joy.

Amen.

Declaration

Speak this aloud:

Obedience leads me into God's joy.

I do not earn reward—I enter it.

My faithfulness draws me closer to God.

Joy grows where alignment remains.

I delight in the Lord.

Commitment to Obedience

Today, I commit to **joy-centered obedience**.

I release expectation of reward as payment

and choose faithfulness as relationship.

Closing Orientation

Joy deepens quietly.

Tomorrow, we will explore **how obedience reshapes our understanding of faith—not as certainty, but as trust that walks forward.**

DAY TWENTY-NINE
Faith That Walks Forward

Why Obedience Does Not Wait for Certainty

KEY FOCUS SCRIPTURES

- **2 Corinthians 5:7** — *For we walk by faith, not by sight.*
- **Hebrews 11:1, 8** — *Faith is confidence in what we hope for... Abraham obeyed and went, even though he did not know where he was going.*
- **Proverbs 3:5–6** — *Trust in the Lord with all your heart...*

Scripture Reading (Read Slowly)
"For we walk by faith, not by sight."
— 2 Corinthians 5:7
Pause.
Notice that faith is described as **movement**, not conclusion.

Devotional Reflection
Many people assume faith requires certainty.

We wait for clarity before we move. We want assurance before obedience. We expect faith to remove ambiguity, questions, and risk. Scripture presents a different pattern: faith often begins **before certainty arrives**.

Faith is not knowing where the path leads.

Faith is trusting the One who leads.

Before **C. S. Lewis** embraced Christian faith fully, one of his greatest struggles was the loss of control. Faith required him to step forward without exhaustive answers. He did not move because every question was resolved; he moved because honesty demanded trust.

This is deeply modern.

We live in a culture that prizes certainty, evidence, and guarantees. Faith disrupts that posture. It does not reject reason—but it refuses to be governed by fear of the unknown. Obedience rooted in faith does not wait for complete understanding. It walks forward with partial light.

Day 29 invites you to examine where you may be waiting for certainty instead of practicing trust.

Faith does not eliminate questions.

It decides despite them.

Obedience is the visible expression of faith. It reveals what we trust more—our understanding or God's faithfulness. When faith is reduced to agreement, it stalls. When faith becomes movement, it grows.

Walking by faith does not mean reckless action.

It means responsive trust.

God often reveals the next step only after obedience is chosen. Faith is formed not in resolution, but in motion.

Heart Examination

Sit with these questions quietly.

1. **Where are you waiting for certainty before obeying?**
2. **What fears surface when clarity feels incomplete?**
3. **What step of trust might God be inviting you to take now?**

Today's Practice (Faith in Motion)

Today's practice is **obedient movement.**

Identify **one small step of obedience** you have delayed because you wanted more clarity.

Take that step today.

Do not rush.

Do not dramatize it.

Just move.

PRAYER

Father,

Teach me faith that walks forward.

Release me from the need for total certainty
and strengthen my trust in You.
Help me obey with the light I have
and trust You to guide the next step.
I place my confidence in You.
Amen.

Declaration

Speak this aloud:
I walk by faith, not by sight.
Obedience does not wait for certainty.
God guides my steps as I move forward.
I trust Him beyond what I understand.
My faith is active and alive.

Commitment to Obedience

Today, I commit to **faith-filled obedience**.
I will not delay alignment
while waiting for perfect clarity.
I choose to trust and move forward.

Closing Orientation

You are nearing the end of the journey.

Tomorrow, we will explore **how obedience reshapes our understanding of completion—not as arrival, but as lifelong faithfulness.**

DAY THIRTY
Faithfulness Without Finish Lines

Why Obedience Is a Way of Life, Not a Destination

KEY FOCUS SCRIPTURES

- **Philippians 3:12–14** — *Not that I have already obtained all this... but I press on.*
- **Luke 9:62** — *No one who puts a hand to the plow and looks back is fit for the kingdom of God.*
- **Hebrews 12:1–2** — *Let us run with perseverance the race marked out for us.*

Scripture Reading (Read Slowly)
"Not that I have already obtained all this,
or have already arrived at my goal,
but I press on..."
— Philippians 3:12
Pause.
Notice that even maturity refuses the language of arrival.

Devotional Reflection
We are tempted to treat obedience as a project.

We look for milestones, markers of completion, moments when we can finally say, *"I've arrived."* Scripture gently dismantles this expectation. The Christian life does not culminate in mastery—it continues in faithfulness.

Completion, in Scripture, is not about having finished becoming.

It is about having remained aligned.

Before **C. S. Lewis** reached the later years of his life, obedience had already taught him something crucial: there is no version of faith where growth stops being required. Even clarity invites deeper surrender. Even maturity demands continued humility.

Paul—one of the most spiritually formed voices in Scripture—refused to speak as though he had arrived. Instead, he pressed on. This posture protects obedience from pride and keeps faith responsive rather than static.

Day 30 invites you to release the idea of completion as arrival.

Obedience does not culminate in comfort.

It settles into **consistency**.

Faithfulness is not dramatic. It is steady. It is choosing alignment again tomorrow. It is continuing the race without applause, without certainty, without the illusion that the work is done.

This is not discouraging.

It is freeing.

You do not need to reach a final version of yourself.

You are invited to remain faithful as you are being formed.

God completes His work not by rushing us to an endpoint, but by sustaining us through the journey.

Heart Examination

Sit with these questions quietly.

1. **Where have you been tempted to measure spiritual life by arrival rather than faithfulness?**
2. **How do you respond to the idea that formation continues for a lifetime?**
3. **What does "pressing on" look like in your life right now?**

Today's Practice (Steady Commitment)

Today's practice is **renewed orientation**.

Pray this slowly:

"Lord, I commit to faithful obedience today—and again tomorrow."

No resolutions.

No finish lines.

Just alignment.

Prayer

Father,

Release me from the illusion of arrival.

Teach me faithfulness that remains steady over time.

Help me press on with humility, endurance, and trust.

I place my hand to the plow

and choose not to look back.

Sustain me as You continue Your work in me.

Amen.

Declaration

Speak this aloud:

I do not live for arrival—I live for alignment.

Obedience is my lifelong calling.

I press on with faithfulness and trust.

God is completing His work in me over time.

I remain steady in the race set before me.

Commitment to Obedience

Today, I commit to **lifelong faithfulness**.

I release the need for completion as arrival

and choose steady obedience as my way of life.

Closing Orientation

This is not an ending.

It is a **settled posture**.

What follows now will not add pressure—

it will deepen practice.

DAY THIRTY-ONE
Your Life as the Text

When Obedience Moves From Reading to Living

K ey Focus Scriptures

- **2 Corinthians 3:2–3** — *You yourselves are our letter... written not with ink but with the Spirit of the living God.*
- **Matthew 7:24–27** — *The wise person puts these words into practice.*
- **James 1:23–25** — *Whoever looks intently... and does not forget but does—will be blessed.*

Scripture Reading (Read Slowly)
"You yourselves are our letter,
written on our hearts,
known and read by everyone."
— 2 Corinthians 3:2
Pause.
Notice **who is being read**.
Devotional Reflection
Up to this point, you have been reading lives, Scripture, and truth.
From here on, **your life becomes the text**.

Christian formation does not end with understanding. It culminates in embodiment. Scripture does not ask whether truth has been admired—it asks whether it has been *lived*. The final measure of this journey is not what you have absorbed, but what has begun to shape your daily choices.

This is where many believers hesitate.

It is safer to read than to practice.

Safer to reflect than to reorder.

Safer to agree than to embody.

Yet Scripture insists that the world encounters Christ not primarily through texts, but through **people**. Through tone, response, patience, restraint, courage, mercy, and faithfulness lived quietly in ordinary places.

Day 31 marks a shift.

You are no longer reading about obedience.

You are being invited to **become readable**.

Your routines, relationships, reactions, and responsibilities now carry weight. The question is no longer *"What does this mean?"* but *"How will this be lived?"*

You do not need a new role or platform.

You need alignment where you already stand.

The Spirit writes most clearly where obedience is practiced consistently—in kitchens, offices, conversations, disappointments, decisions no one else notices. This is where living epistles are formed.

From this point forward, each day will present **a lived scenario**, not a lesson. You are not asked to analyze it. You are asked to inhabit it.

Heart Examination

Sit with these questions quietly.

1. **Where is your life already being "read" by others?**
2. **What patterns in your daily life most clearly communicate your faith?**
3. **What would it mean to live with awareness that your life is a witness?**

Today's Practice (Intentional Visibility)

Today's practice is **conscious alignment**.

Choose **one ordinary setting** you will enter today—work, home, conversation, errand.

Before entering it, pray:

"Lord, let my life be readable here."

Then proceed normally—but attentively.

Prayer

Father,
I offer You my ordinary life.
Teach me to live in a way that reflects truth
without performance or pretense.
Write Your grace into my actions,
my words, and my responses.
Let my life speak quietly and clearly.
Amen.

Declaration

Speak this aloud:
My life is a living letter of Christ.
God's Spirit is writing through my obedience.
I live attentively and faithfully.
My daily life bears witness to truth.
I am becoming readable to the world.

Commitment to Obedience

Today, I commit to **living intentionally**.
I choose awareness over autopilot
and alignment over invisibility.

Closing Orientation

From here forward, the focus narrows.
Not toward theology,
but toward **practice**.

Tomorrow, we will explore **how obedience is revealed through our responses under pressure**.

DAY THIRTY-TWO
What Emerges Under Pressure

How Obedience Is Revealed When Control Is Lost

Key Focus Scriptures

- **Luke 6:43–45** — *Out of the overflow of the heart the mouth speaks.*
- **Proverbs 4:23** — *Guard your heart, for everything you do flows from it.*
- **1 Peter 1:6–7** — *Trials come so that the genuineness of your faith may be proved.*

Scripture Reading (Read Slowly)
"For the mouth speaks what the heart is full of."
— Luke 6:45
Pause.
Notice that pressure does not create content—it **reveals** it.

Devotional Reflection
Pressure is a revealer.

It does not invent new reactions; it exposes existing formation. When control is lost—through stress, interruption, conflict, or disappointment—what surfaces shows us what obedience has been shaping beneath the surface.

This is uncomfortable, but it is also clarifying.

We often judge ourselves by intention. God forms us through **response**. Under pressure, intention gives way to instinct. And instinct tells the truth about what has taken root.

Day 32 invites you to see pressure not as an enemy, but as information.

If impatience surfaces, it reveals where hurry still governs.

If defensiveness rises, it reveals where control still grips.

If gentleness appears, it reveals where obedience has quietly done its work.

Pressure does not mean failure.

It means exposure.

God uses pressure to bring alignment into focus—not to shame us, but to show us where formation is still unfolding. These moments are invitations, not indictments.

You are not asked to eliminate pressure.

You are invited to learn from it.

When obedience has shaped the heart, pressure becomes a witness. It shows the world what governs you when circumstances do not cooperate.

Heart Examination

Sit with these questions quietly.

1. **What reactions tend to surface when you are under pressure?**
2. **What do those reactions reveal about what is still being formed?**
3. **How might pressure become a teacher rather than a threat?**

Today's Practice (Attentive Response)

Today's practice is **slow response under pressure**.

When something disrupts your plans today—a delay, frustration, interruption—pause before responding.

Take one breath.

Then choose a response aligned with truth rather than impulse.

Do not aim for perfection.

Aim for awareness.

PRAYER

Father,

Thank You for showing me what pressure reveals.

Teach me to respond rather than react.

Use moments of strain to deepen my alignment,

not to discourage my obedience.

Form my heart where control is tested.

Amen.

Declaration

Speak this aloud:

Pressure reveals what God is forming in me.

I respond with awareness, not impulse.

Obedience shapes my reactions under strain.

God uses pressure to deepen alignment.

I remain steady when control is tested.

Commitment to Obedience

Today, I commit to **attentive response**.

I will not fear pressure

or hide from what it reveals.

I allow God to use it for formation.

Closing Orientation

Pressure does not undo formation.

It **discloses** it.

Tomorrow, we will explore **how obedience is revealed through consistency in small, repeated choices.**

DAY THIRTY-THREE
Formed by What You Repeat

Why Obedience Is Built Through Small, Faithful Choices

Key Focus Scriptures

- **Luke 16:10** — *Whoever is faithful in very little is faithful also in much.*
- **Galatians 6:7–9** — *Do not grow weary in doing good...*
- **Psalm 1:1–3** — *That person is like a tree planted by streams of water...*

Scripture Reading (Read Slowly)
"Whoever is faithful in very little
is faithful also in much."
— Luke 16:10
Pause.
Notice that faithfulness is measured **over time**, not in moments.

Devotional Reflection
Most formation happens quietly.

Not in decisive moments, but in repeated ones. Not through dramatic obedience, but through consistent alignment. Scripture repeatedly affirms this truth: who we are becoming is shaped more by what we do **often** than by what we do **occasionally**.

We tend to overestimate the power of a single choice and underestimate the power of repetition.

Obedience, practiced consistently, becomes character. Small acts, repeated daily, form patterns that eventually feel natural. This is how alignment settles into the body and the will—not through intensity, but through faithfulness.

Day 33 invites you to look honestly at your rhythms.

Consistency reveals allegiance.

What you repeat reveals what governs you. Over time, repeated obedience stabilizes desire, reshapes instinct, and anchors response. This is why Scripture compares the faithful person to a tree—rooted, nourished, steady. Growth is slow, but it is certain.

Consistency also protects us from discouragement.

When we look for progress only in dramatic change, we miss what is quietly forming. God often works beneath visibility, strengthening roots before producing fruit. Repetition trains trust. It allows obedience to outlast emotion, motivation, and mood.

You do not need extraordinary obedience today.

You need faithful repetition.

Heart Examination

Sit with these questions quietly.

1. **What small choices do you repeat most consistently each day?**
2. **Which habits are currently shaping your character—intentionally or unintentionally?**
3. **Where might God be inviting you to practice quiet faithfulness rather than dramatic change?**

Today's Practice (Faithful Repetition)

Today's practice is **one repeated act.**

Choose **one small act of obedience** you can repeat daily—prayer, Scripture reading, kindness, restraint, gratitude.

Do it today **without embellishment.**

Then commit to repeating it tomorrow.

Prayer

Father,

Teach me to value faithfulness over intensity.

Help me trust the quiet power of obedience repeated over time.

Form my character through steady alignment,

and strengthen my resolve to remain faithful in small things.

I offer You my consistency.

Amen.

Declaration

Speak this aloud:

God forms my life through faithful repetition.

Small acts of obedience shape lasting character.

I remain steady in alignment.

What I repeat reflects my allegiance.

I grow rooted, patient, and faithful.

Commitment to Obedience

Today, I commit to **consistent faithfulness**.

I choose repeated obedience

over occasional intensity.

Closing Orientation

Formation deepens through repetition.

Tomorrow, we will explore **how obedience is revealed through restraint—what we choose not to do.**

DAY THIRTY-FOUR
The Obedience of Restraint

Why What You Refuse Matters as Much as What You Choose

K ey Focus Scriptures

- **Titus 2:11–12** — *Grace teaches us to say "No" to ungodliness...*
- **Proverbs 25:28** — *Like a city whose walls are broken through is a person who lacks self-control.*
- **1 Corinthians 6:12** — *"I have the right to do anything," you say—but not everything is beneficial.*

Scripture Reading (Read Slowly)
"The grace of God... teaches us to say 'No.'"
— Titus 2:12
Pause.
Notice that restraint is not law—it is **grace-trained**.

Devotional Reflection
Much of obedience is invisible.

We often associate obedience with action—speaking, serving, choosing, moving. Scripture reveals another form that is quieter and just as formative: **restraint**. Obedience is sometimes expressed not by what we pursue, but by what we decline.

Restraint protects formation.

Not everything permissible is beneficial. Not every opportunity is aligned. Not every impulse deserves expression. Grace teaches us discernment—the wisdom to say no without fear and without pride.

This kind of obedience rarely receives affirmation. No one applauds what you did not say, the argument you did not escalate, the opportunity you declined, the impulse you restrained. Yet these moments shape character deeply.

Day 34 invites you to recognize restraint as spiritual maturity.

Restraint is not weakness.

It is strength under control.

It reflects a life no longer governed by impulse or pressure, but by alignment. When obedience has settled deeply, restraint becomes natural—not forced. We learn to pause, discern, and choose silence or refusal when alignment requires it.

What you refuse reveals what governs you.

A person unable to say no is not free. A person trained by grace knows when restraint protects peace, integrity, and love. This kind of obedience guards the inner life and preserves fruit already formed.

Heart Examination

Sit with these questions quietly.

1. **Where do you find it hardest to practice restraint—speech, reaction, desire, opportunity?**
2. **What fears surface when you consider saying no?**
3. **How might restraint serve alignment rather than limit it?**

Today's Practice (Intentional Restraint)

Today's practice is **a chosen no.**

Pay attention for **one moment today** where you feel the urge to react, respond immediately, or say yes automatically.

Pause.

Choose restraint.

It may be silence.

It may be delay.

It may be refusal.

Let alignment lead.

Prayer

Father,

Teach me obedience that includes restraint.

Help me recognize when saying no

protects what You are forming in me.

Train my desires through grace,

and give me wisdom to choose alignment over impulse.

I trust You with what I release.

Amen.

Declaration

Speak this aloud:

God's grace trains my restraint.

I am not governed by impulse.

Obedience shapes what I refuse as well as what I choose.

I act with wisdom and self-control.

My life is guarded by alignment.

Commitment to Obedience

Today, I commit to **grace-filled restraint**.

I choose alignment over impulse

and wisdom over reaction.

Closing Orientation

Restraint protects formation.

Tomorrow, we will explore **how obedience is revealed through forgiveness—especially when it costs something**.

DAY THIRTY-FIVE
The Cost of Forgiveness

Why Obedience Sometimes Requires Letting Go Without Resolution

Key Focus Scriptures

- **Matthew 18:21–22** — *How many times shall I forgive?*
- **Ephesians 4:31–32** — *Forgiving one another, just as in Christ God forgave you.*
- **Romans 12:19** — *Do not avenge yourselves...*

Scripture Reading (Read Slowly)
"Forgive as the Lord forgave you."
— Ephesians 4:32
Pause.
Notice the standard—not fairness, but Christ.

Devotional Reflection
Forgiveness is one of the most misunderstood acts of obedience.

We often treat forgiveness as emotional resolution—waiting until pain subsides, trust is restored, or justice feels complete. Scripture defines forgiveness differently. Forgiveness is an act of obedience that **releases the right to control outcome.**

Forgiveness does not deny harm.

It does not excuse injustice.

It does not require reconciliation.

It releases ownership of judgment.

This makes forgiveness costly.

To forgive is to let go of leverage. To forgive is to refuse to weaponize memory. To forgive is to trust God with what we cannot resolve ourselves. This kind of obedience does not feel freeing at first—it feels like loss.

Yet Scripture insists it is the path to freedom.

Day 35 invites you to see forgiveness not as something you feel ready for, but as something you may be called to **choose**. Forgiveness is not agreement with what happened. It is alignment with God's character in the face of what happened.

Obedience here is quiet and unseen.

No one applauds forgiveness when it costs dignity, pride, or the illusion of control. Yet this is where formation deepens. Forgiveness breaks cycles of resentment that obedience elsewhere cannot reach.

Forgiveness is not forgetting.

It is surrendering the right to retaliate.

This obedience is often repeated—not once, but many times. Forgiveness may need to be chosen again and again, especially when memory resurfaces. Each choice releases a little more control and restores a little more peace.

Heart Examination

Sit with these questions quietly.

1. **Where have you equated forgiveness with emotional readiness?**
2. **Who or what might God be inviting you to release—not resolve—right now?**
3. **What control are you holding onto that forgiveness would require you to surrender?**

Today's Practice (Release Without Resolution)

Today's practice is **intentional release**.

Bring **one unresolved offense** before God—small or significant.

Pray this honestly:

"Lord, I release my right to control this."

Do not force feeling.

Do not rush peace.

Just release.

Prayer

Father,

You see the cost of forgiveness.

You know where obedience feels heavy.

Teach me to release control without bitterness

and to trust You with what I cannot fix.

I choose forgiveness as alignment,

not as denial.

Amen.

Declaration

Speak this aloud:

I forgive as Christ forgave me.

Obedience releases control.

I refuse bitterness and retaliation.

God is my defender and judge.

I walk in freedom through forgiveness.

Commitment to Obedience

Today, I commit to **obedient forgiveness**.

I release my right to control outcomes

and trust God with justice and healing.

Closing Orientation

Forgiveness frees the soul.

Tomorrow, we will explore **how obedience is revealed through humility—especially when pride feels justified**.

DAY THIRTY-SIX
The Obedience of Humility

Why Letting Go of Pride Protects Formation

Key Focus Scriptures

- **Philippians 2:5–8** — *He humbled Himself by becoming obedient to death...*
- **James 4:6** — *God opposes the proud but shows favor to the humble.*
- **Proverbs 11:2** — *When pride comes, then comes disgrace, but with humility comes wisdom.*

Scripture Reading (Read Slowly)
"He humbled Himself
by becoming obedient..."
— Philippians 2:8
Pause.
Notice that humility is **chosen**, not assumed.
Devotional Reflection
Humility is often misunderstood as thinking less of oneself.
Scripture defines humility differently. Humility is not self-erasure; it is **freedom from self-protection**. It is obedience that no longer needs to assert, defend, or dominate in order to feel secure.
Pride resists obedience subtly.
It does not always look arrogant. Often it appears as justification—*I deserve this, I'm right, They should know better*. Pride insists on being seen, validated, or proven correct. Humility releases that demand.
This is costly.

Humility asks us to relinquish the right to be understood, applauded, or vindicated. It does not deny truth; it trusts God with its defense. This posture feels risky because it removes our usual strategies for control.

Yet Scripture is clear: humility attracts grace.

Where pride strains obedience, humility strengthens it. It creates space for correction without collapse, for service without resentment, for obedience without performance.

Day 36 invites you to examine where pride may be quietly resisting formation.

Pride often hides behind competence.

Humility rests in alignment.

Jesus did not humble Himself because He was weak. He humbled Himself because He was secure. His obedience flowed from identity, not insecurity. This is the humility Scripture calls us toward—not shrinking back, but releasing self-importance.

Humility does not diminish you.

It frees you.

Heart Examination

Sit with these questions quietly.

1. **Where do you feel most tempted to defend yourself or prove your worth?**
2. **What situations trigger pride disguised as justification?**
3. **How might humility protect obedience in your current season?**

Today's Practice (Chosen Humility)

Today's practice is **unasserted alignment**.

Notice **one moment today** where you feel the urge to:

- Correct someone
- Defend your position
- Make sure you are seen or credited

Pause.

Choose humility.

You may remain silent.
You may let God defend truth in time.

Prayer

Father,
Teach me humility that releases control.
Free me from the need to defend myself
and help me trust You with my reputation.
Form in me the humility of Christ—
secure, obedient, and free.
I choose alignment over pride.
Amen.

Declaration

Speak this aloud:
I walk in the humility of Christ.
Obedience releases my need for self-defense.
God opposes pride and gives grace to the humble.
I trust God with my reputation.
Humility strengthens my obedience.

Commitment to Obedience

Today, I commit to **humble obedience**.
I release pride, justification, and self-protection
and choose alignment rooted in trust.

Closing Orientation

Humility protects formation.

Tomorrow, we will explore **how obedience is revealed through perseverance—when obedience feels long and unseen.**

DAY THIRTY-SEVEN
When Obedience Must Endure

Why Perseverance Is the Quiet Mark of Maturity

K ey Focus Scriptures

- **Hebrews 10:36** — *You need to persevere so that when you have done the will of God, you will receive what He has promised.*
- **James 5:7–8** — *Be patient... establish your hearts.*
- **Galatians 6:9** — *Let us not grow weary in doing good...*

Scripture Reading (Read Slowly)
"You need to persevere
so that when you have done the will of God,
you will receive what He has promised."
— Hebrews 10:36
Pause.
Notice that perseverance follows obedience—not before it.
Devotional Reflection
Some forms of obedience are brief.
Others require **endurance**.
Perseverance is obedience stretched over time—faithfulness that continues without visible reward, emotional reinforcement, or external confirmation. It is one of the clearest signs of spiritual maturity, precisely because it is rarely dramatic.
Most people can obey briefly.
Few learn to remain faithful consistently.
Perseverance tests motive.

When obedience is energized by novelty, momentum carries it for a while. When novelty fades and momentum slows, perseverance reveals whether obedience was rooted in alignment or emotion. This is where many believers quietly disengage—not through rebellion, but through weariness.

Scripture speaks directly to this moment: *Do not grow weary in doing good.*

Weariness does not mean obedience was wrong.

It often means obedience has been long.

Day 37 invites you to honor the faithfulness that feels ordinary and unseen. God does not measure obedience by intensity alone. He honors endurance—the willingness to remain aligned when the journey feels repetitive or lonely.

Perseverance is not stubbornness.

It is trust extended over time.

It says: *I will continue even when clarity delays.*

I will remain faithful even when affirmation is absent.

I will trust God's promises without needing immediate evidence.

This kind of obedience shapes depth.

What perseverance forms cannot be rushed. It stabilizes character, anchors hope, and protects obedience from collapse when circumstances change.

Heart Examination

Sit with these questions quietly.

1. **Where do you feel weary in your obedience right now?**
2. **What tempts you to disengage—not loudly, but quietly?**
3. **How might perseverance itself be the work God is doing in this season?**

Today's Practice (Enduring Faithfulness)

Today's practice is **continued obedience**.

Choose **one act of obedience** you have been practicing faithfully—even when it feels repetitive or unnoticed.

Do it again today.

Not with enthusiasm.

With resolve.

Prayer

Father,
Strengthen me where obedience feels long.
Guard me from weariness that quietly pulls me away.
Help me remain faithful when results delay
and encouragement is scarce.
I trust that You see what is unseen
and honor what endures.
Amen.

Declaration

Speak this aloud:
I persevere in obedience.
God strengthens me when faithfulness feels long.
I do not grow weary in doing good.
My endurance is forming maturity.
I remain aligned until God completes His work.

Commitment to Obedience

Today, I commit to **enduring obedience**.
I choose faithfulness over fatigue
and trust God with the timing of fruit.

Closing Orientation

Perseverance carries obedience
where emotion cannot.

Tomorrow, we will explore **how obedience reshapes our relationship with hope for others—not just ourselves.**

DAY THIRTY-EIGHT
Obedience That Carries Others

Why Formation Always Expands Beyond You

K ey Focus Scriptures

- **Galatians 6:2** — *Carry each other's burdens, and in this way you will fulfill the law of Christ.*
- **Romans 15:1** — *We who are strong ought to bear with the failings of the weak.*
- **Colossians 1:9–10** — *We continually ask God to fill you with the knowledge of His will...*

Scripture Reading (Read Slowly)
"Carry each other's burdens,
and in this way you will fulfill the law of Christ."
— Galatians 6:2
Pause.
Notice that maturity expresses itself through **responsibility for others**.

Devotional Reflection
Formation is never meant to terminate in the self.

As obedience matures, its direction changes. What began as personal alignment expands into concern, patience, prayer, and endurance **for others**. This is not because others become our responsibility to fix, but because love reshapes our posture toward them.

Obedience that remains inward eventually stagnates.

Obedience that turns outward multiplies.

Day 38 invites you to recognize a quiet shift: as God steadies your life, He also enlarges your capacity to carry others—not with solutions, but with presence. Not with control, but with compassion.

Carrying others does not mean absorbing their burdens.

It means walking alongside them faithfully.

This kind of obedience is patient. It resists judgment. It does not rush growth or demand change. It trusts that God is working in others just as He has been working in you—often slowly, often invisibly.

Mature obedience creates space.

Space for people to struggle without being dismissed.

Space for weakness without condemnation.

Space for hope to grow without pressure.

This is why Scripture connects obedience with prayer for others. Intercession is obedience expressed through love. It acknowledges that transformation belongs to God, not us.

Day 38 shifts the question from *"How am I being formed?"* to *"Who might God be inviting me to carry with grace?"*

Heart Examination

Sit with these questions quietly.

1. **Who comes to mind when you think about someone needing patience or prayer?**
2. **Where have you felt tempted to withdraw rather than carry others?**
3. **How might obedience express itself through compassion rather than correction?**

Today's Practice (Intercessory Obedience)

Today's practice is **intentional prayer for another**.

Choose **one person**—someone struggling, distant, or difficult.

Pray for them **without agenda**:

- Not for change
- Not for resolution
- Simply for God's presence and grace in their life

Carry them quietly today.

Prayer

Father,

Thank You for expanding my obedience beyond myself.

Teach me to carry others with humility and grace.

Release me from judgment and control

and form compassion that reflects Your heart.

I trust You to work in others as You have worked in me.

Amen.

Declaration

Speak this aloud:

My obedience carries compassion for others.

I bear burdens with patience and grace.

God works through my prayers and presence.

I walk alongside others without judgment.

Love expands what obedience has formed.

Commitment to Obedience

Today, I commit to **outward-facing obedience**.

I choose compassion over withdrawal

and prayer over control.

Closing Orientation

Obedience widens as it matures.

Tomorrow, we will explore **how obedience prepares us to release control completely—into God's hands**.

DAY THIRTY-NINE
The Obedience of Release

When Faith Places the Outcome Fully in God's Hands

KEY FOCUS SCRIPTURES

- **Psalm 37:5** — *Commit your way to the Lord; trust in Him, and He will act.*
- **Matthew 16:24–25** — *Whoever loses their life for Me will find it.*
- **1 Peter 5:6–7** — *Humble yourselves... casting all your anxieties on Him.*

Scripture Reading (Read Slowly)
"Commit your way to the Lord;
trust in Him,
and He will act."
— Psalm 37:5
Pause.
Notice the sequence: **commit → trust → release**.
Devotional Reflection
Much of obedience is about choosing.
Day 39 is about **releasing**.
There comes a point in formation where effort no longer deepens alignment. Trying harder does not produce peace. Pushing further does not bring clarity. Obedience reaches its maturity when it learns how to **let go**.

Release is not abandonment.

It is trust without leverage.

We often obey while quietly managing outcomes—hoping to influence results, timelines, or responses. We follow God, but keep one hand on control. Day 39 invites you to notice what you are still holding.

Release is one of the hardest forms of obedience because it removes our final safety net.

It means trusting God not only with direction, but with consequences. It means surrendering the need to understand how obedience will be rewarded or recognized. It means resting in faithfulness even when results remain unseen.

Release does not mean passivity.

It means relinquishing ownership of outcome.

This posture reflects deep maturity. It echoes the prayer of Christ Himself: *"Not my will, but Yours be done."* Obedience culminates not in certainty, but in surrender.

Day 39 asks a gentle but penetrating question:

Can you obey without needing to know what happens next?

This is where peace begins to settle—not because everything is resolved, but because trust has replaced control. Release allows God to work without interference. It creates space for grace to move freely.

Heart Examination

Sit with these questions quietly.

1. **What outcome are you still trying to manage?**
2. **Where do you feel anxious about what obedience might cost or produce?**
3. **What would it look like to place this fully in God's hands?**

Today's Practice (Intentional Release)

Today's practice is **named surrender**.

Identify **one specific concern, outcome, or future question** you have been carrying.

Name it before God.

Then pray:

"Lord, I release this to You.

I trust You with the outcome."
Do not revisit it today.

Prayer
Father,
Teach me obedience that knows when to release.
Free me from managing what belongs to You.
Help me trust You beyond understanding,
beyond timelines, beyond outcomes.
I place my life, my future, and my faith
fully in Your hands.
Amen.

Declaration
Speak this aloud:
I release control and trust God fully.
Obedience does not require ownership of outcome.
God is faithful with what I surrender.
I walk in peace, not anxiety.
My life rests in God's hands.

Commitment to Obedience
Today, I commit to **obedient release**.
I place outcomes, timing, and results
fully in God's care.

Closing Orientation
Tomorrow is not a conclusion.
It is a **commissioning**.
Day 40 will not ask you to do more.
It will invite you to **live from what has been formed**.

DAY FORTY
Sent as a Living Epistle

When Formation Becomes Witness

Key Focus Scriptures

- **2 Corinthians 3:2–3** — *You are a letter from Christ... written by the Spirit of the living God.*
- **Matthew 5:16** — *Let your light shine before others...*
- **John 20:21** — *As the Father has sent Me, I am sending you.*

Scripture Reading (Read Slowly)
"You yourselves are our letter,
written on our hearts,
known and read by everyone."
— 2 Corinthians 3:2
Pause.
Notice that the letter is **not sealed**.
It is **read daily**.
Devotional Reflection
This is not the end.
It is the point where reading becomes living.

For forty days, you have allowed truth to confront, align, refine, and release you. You have examined obedience not as performance, but as posture. You have seen that faith matures through restraint, forgiveness, humility, perseverance, compassion, and surrender.

Now comes the quiet question Scripture always asks last:
What will be read in your life next?

God does not finish His work in you by closing a book.
He finishes it by **sending you back into ordinary life—changed**.
A living epistle is not written for admiration.
It is written for witness.
Your tone in conversation.
Your patience under pressure.
Your restraint when provoked.
Your forgiveness when wronged.
Your faithfulness when unseen.
These are the pages the world reads.
You are not commissioned to explain Christ exhaustively.
You are commissioned to **embody Him faithfully**.
This does not require a platform.
It requires alignment.

The Spirit writes through lives yielded over time. Through consistency more than intensity. Through obedience more than articulation. Through love that remains steady when circumstances fluctuate.

Day 40 does not send you out with urgency.
It sends you out with **clarity**.
You are not becoming something new tomorrow.
You are continuing what has already begun.

Final Heart Examination

Sit with these questions slowly.

1. **What has shifted in you over these forty days?**
2. **Where do you sense God inviting you to live more attentively?**
3. **What part of your ordinary life now feels newly significant?**

Today's Practice (Commissioned Living)

Today's practice is **intentional embodiment**.

Choose one simple posture to carry forward:

- attentiveness
- restraint
- patience

- humility
- faithfulness

Do not announce it.
Do not measure it.
Just live it.

Prayer of Commissioning

Father,
Thank You for the work You have done within me.
I offer You my life—not as performance,
but as a living witness to Your grace.
Send me into ordinary spaces with quiet faithfulness.
Let my life reflect Christ clearly,
consistently, and truthfully.
I receive Your sending.
Amen.

Final Declaration

Speak this aloud:
I am a living epistle of Christ.
God's Spirit is writing through my obedience.
I live with clarity, faithfulness, and humility.
My life bears witness to truth.
I am sent.

Final Commitment

I commit to **living what has been formed**.
I will not rush past obedience
or reduce faith to ideas.
I offer my life as a readable witness of Christ.

A Closing Word

You have not completed a program.
You have entered a posture.
Read slowly.
Obey quietly.
Live clearly.
The world is reading.

— Living Epistles

CONCLUSION
When the Reading Ends, the Writing Continues

This book was never meant to be finished in the usual sense.

It was meant to **finish something in you**—and then begin something through you.

You have not merely walked through forty days of reflection. You have been invited into a posture: a way of seeing obedience not as obligation, but as alignment; not as performance, but as formation; not as information, but as embodiment.

From the life and witness of C. S. Lewis, you have seen that belief alone does not transform a person. Understanding does not automatically yield obedience. Even sincerity does not substitute for surrender. Transformation happens when truth moves from the mind into the will—and from the will into daily life.

This is the quiet miracle of formation.

You have traced a journey from reluctance to yielding, from admiration to obedience, from inward wrestling to outward witness. Along the way, you have encountered questions that could not be answered quickly, practices that required restraint, and moments that asked you to trust without control.

That was intentional.

Because God does not write His clearest work through speed.

He writes through faithfulness.

A living epistle is not produced in a moment. It is written line by line—through repeated obedience, quiet surrender, unseen perseverance, and love practiced in ordinary spaces. It is read not by those who admire us, but by those who live alongside us.

Your life is now the text.

Not a perfect one.

Not a finished one.

But a truthful one.

You are not sent out as an expert.

You are sent out as a witness.

You are not commissioned to explain everything.

You are commissioned to **live clearly**.

The Spirit of God continues to write—not with ink, not with argument, not with noise—but through your responses under pressure, your restraint when provoked, your forgiveness when wronged, your humility when unseen, and your faithfulness when obedience feels long.

This is how Christ is made visible.

As you close this book, resist the temptation to move on too quickly. Do not look for the next program, the next voice, or the next insight to replace what has begun. Let what has been formed take root. Let obedience settle into habit. Let faithfulness become unremarkable and steady.

Read slowly.

Obey quietly.

Live clearly.

The world is still reading.

And the Author is still writing.

CALL TO ACTION

A Partnership for the Harvest

As you close this book, we invite you to carry the journey one step further—not only in your own life, but into the lives of countless souls across the nations.

If the messages from God's Eagle Ministries (GEM) have strengthened, awakened, or realigned your heart, we humbly ask you to prayerfully consider **partnering with us for the sake of the harvest**. The world is hungry for truth, hope, and the gentle yet unmistakable voice of the Holy Spirit, and together we can place these messages where they are needed most.

We believe media is more than technology—it is a **spiritual net** cast deep into nations, villages, cities, and hidden places. Through film, video, radio, and digital ministry, GEM is reaching people who may never enter a church, but whose hearts are wide open to encounter the living Christ.

Your partnership helps us:

1. Produce Spirit-Filled Film & Video Content

Stories and teachings that heal, inspire, and reveal the love of Jesus in clear, relatable, life-changing ways.

2. Broadcast the Gospel on Radio

Carrying God's Word into prisons, hospitals, rural communities, and places far beyond internet reach—where hope is scarce and truth is precious.

3. Expand Our Social Media Teaching & Discipleship Campaigns

Daily devotionals, prayers, and teachings that strengthen believers, restore families, and equip disciples globally.

Why Your Support Matters

EVERY MESSAGE RELEASED becomes a seed of light.

Every teaching becomes a ripple of transformation.

Every act of generosity becomes part of God's global harvest.

Your giving helps this ministry reach souls we may never meet on earth, but will surely meet in eternity. There is no fixed amount—give only as the Lord leads you. Every gift, large or small, plays a part in advancing the Kingdom.

To Partner or Give:

PayPal:

https://www.paypal.com/ncp/payment/D6NEFW56KG8LU

Tithe.ly:

https://tithe.ly/give?c=308311

Flutterwave – https://flutterwave.com/donate/bbkpkokehxlw

ALL GIVING AVENUES:

https://www.otakada.org/partnership-giving

Thank you for standing with us.

Thank you for sowing into the harvest.

Thank you for helping us bring the message of Christ to the nations.

May the Lord bless you richly, increase you abundantly, and multiply every seed you sow for His glory.

In Jesus' mighty name, Amen.

—Ambassador Monday O. Ogbe, Zacharias Godseagle; Comfort Ladi Ogbe

Founder, God's Eagle Ministries (GEM)

www.otakada.org[1]

---

1.   http://www.otakada.org

How to Be Born Again and Start a New Life with Christ

M aybe you've walked with Jesus before, or maybe you've just met Him through these 40 days. But right now, something inside you is stirring.

You're ready for more than religion.

You're ready for **relationship**.

You're ready to say, "Jesus, I need You."

Here's the truth:

"For everyone has sinned; we all fall short of God's glorious standard... yet God, in His grace, freely makes us right in His sight."

— Romans 3:23–24 (NLT)

You can't earn salvation.

You can't fix yourself.

But Jesus already paid the full price — and He's waiting to welcome you home.

How to Be Born Again

Being born again means surrendering your life to Jesus — accepting His forgiveness, believing He died and rose again, and receiving Him as your Lord and Savior.

It's simple. It's powerful. It changes everything.

Pray This Out Loud:

"Lord Jesus, I believe You are the Son of God.

I believe You died for my sins and rose again.

I confess that I have sinned and I need Your forgiveness.

Today, I repent and turn from my old ways.

I invite You into my life to be my Lord and Savior.

Wash me clean. Fill me with Your Spirit.

I declare I am born again, forgiven, and free.

**From this day forward, I will follow You —
and I will live in Your steps.
Thank You for saving me. In Jesus' name, amen."**
Next Steps After Salvation

1. **Tell Someone** – Share your decision with a believer you trust.
2. **Find a Bible-Based Church** – Join a community that teaches God's Word and lives it out. Visit God's Eagle ministries online via https://www.otakada.org or https://chat.whatsapp.com/ H67spSun32DDTma8TLh0ov
3. **Get Baptized** – Take the next step publicly to declare your faith.
4. **Read the Bible Daily** – Start with the Gospel of John.
5. **Pray Every Day** – Talk to God as a friend and Father.
6. **Stay Connected** – Surround yourself with people who encourage your new walk.
7. **Start a discipleship Process within the community** – Develop one on one relationship with Jesus Christ via these links

40-day discipleship 1 - https://www.otakada.org/get-free-40-days-online-discipleship-course-in-a-journey-with-jesus/

40 Discipleship 2 - https://www.otakada.org/get-free-40-days-dna-of-discipleship-journey-with-jesus-series-2/

My Salvation Moment

Date: _____

Signature: _____

"If anyone is in Christ, he is a new creation; the old has passed away, the new has come!"

— 2 Corinthians 5:17

Certificate of New Life in Christ

SALVATION DECLARATION – Born Again by Grace

This certifies that

_____

(Full Name)

has publicly declared **faith in Jesus Christ**

as Lord and Savior and has received the free gift of salvation

through His death and resurrection.

"If you openly declare that Jesus is Lord and believe in your heart that God raised Him from the dead, you will be saved."

— Romans 10:9 (NLT)

On this day, heaven rejoices and a new journey begins.

Date of Decision: _____

Signature: _____

Salvation Declaration

"Today, I surrender my life to Jesus Christ.

I believe He died for my sins and rose again.

I receive Him as my Lord and Savior.

I am forgiven, born again, and made new.

From this moment forward, I will walk in His steps."

Welcome to the Family of God!

Your name is written in the Lamb's Book of Life.

Your story is just beginning — and it's eternal.

CONNECT WITH GOD'S EAGLE MINISTRIES

- Website: www.otakada.org[1]
- Wealth Beyond Worry Series: www.wealthbeyondworryseries.com[2]
- Email: ambassador@otakada.org

- **Support this work:**

SUPPORT KINGDOM PROJECTS, missions, and free global resources through covenant-led giving.
Scan QR Code to Give
https://tithe.ly/give?c=308311
Your generosity helps us reach more souls, translate resources, support missionaries, and build discipleship systems globally. Thank you!

---

1. https://www.otakada.org
2. https://www.wealthbeyondworryseries.com

Author BIO

Zacharias Godseagle

Author • **Teacher** • **Visionary Leader**
Zacharias Godseagle is a passionate teacher of the Word and a discerning voice to the Body of Christ. Carrying a unique grace for spiritual insight, Zacharias ministers with clarity, prophetic depth, and a heart-burning desire to see believers walk in purity, godliness, and authentic surrender to Christ.

As a co-laborer in the work of God's Eagle Ministries (GEM), he plays a significant role in shaping discipleship content, scriptural illumination, and media-based outreach that touches lives across digital and physical frontiers. His writings focus on inner transformation, obedience, and the restoration of Christ to the throne of the believer's heart.

Zacharias is driven by a simple conviction: **when the heart is aligned, destiny aligns.**

He continues to reach audiences globally through teaching, mentorship, and Spirit-filled creative projects.

Ambassador Monday O. Ogbe

AUTHOR • **MISSIONARY** Communicator • Founder, God's Eagle Ministries (GEM)

Ambassador Monday Oreojo Ogwuojo Ogbe is the founder of **God's Eagle Ministries (GEM)**—a global mission with a mandate to "connect people to God through His Word." Known for his intense passion for truth, emotional storytelling, and prophetic teaching, he ministers across nations through writing, podcasting, filmmaking, digital evangelism, and discipleship.

With a background in leadership, media, and missions, Ambassador Monday carries a cross-cultural anointing that resonates from Africa to Asia, the Americas, Europe, and the Middle East. His teachings confront the hidden battles of the believer's heart—covetousness, identity struggles, spiritual complacency, and the subtle erosion of intimacy with God.

He is the author of numerous devotionals, book series, and multimedia teachings that reach millions through otakada.org and GEM's digital platforms.

His life message is simple but profound:

"When Christ sits at the center, everything else takes its rightful place."

Comfort Ladi Ogbe

AUTHOR • INTERCESSOR • Co-Laborer in Ministry

Comfort Ladi Ogbe is a writer, intercessor, and co-laborer in the Kingdom assignment of God's Eagle Ministries. Gifted with compassion, discernment, and a nurturing spirit, she brings emotional depth and spiritual grounding to every project she touches.

Her contributions—often behind the scenes—carry the fragrance of humility, wisdom, and healing. Comfort ministers through counseling, prayer, discipleship, and creative collaboration, especially in works that emphasize family restoration, spiritual maturity, and heart transformation.

As an author, she writes from a place of lived experience and spiritual conviction, offering readers clarity, comfort, and encouragement to pursue wholeness in Christ.

Comfort is committed to helping believers experience God not only in knowledge, but in daily life—where the heart learns to trust, surrender, and flourish.

Author Page:

https://www.amazon.com/stores/Zacharias-Godseagle/author/B0FCZ89D4K

RECOMMENDED BOOKS & RESOURCES

ST. AUGUSTINE OF HIPPO (354–430 AD)
From a Restless Heart to a Written Life - Living Epistles – 40 Day
Devotional Series - 1

Amazon Ebook link - https://www.amazon.com/ST-AUGUSTINE-
HIPPO-354-430-Devotional-ebook/dp/B0GJN8N9XS
Amazon Paperback order link - https://www.amazon.com/St-Augustine-
Hippo-354-430-Devotional/dp/B0GJWTVLR6

Ingramspark Paperback Link - https://shop.ingramspark.com/b/
084?params=BZOOW3dj93aGEtBL2Fv1VY8wV1OQvA10dtZRDgk7Z9Z
SCAN ME

RENEWAL 7
Heal the Heart of Your Home in 7 Days
The Renewal Series – Family Unity Edition

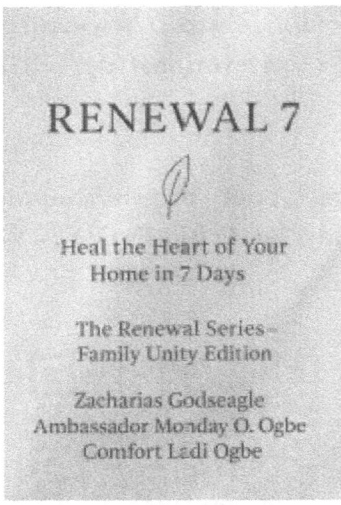

Link to Book Paperback - https://shop.ingramspark.com/b/084?params=htyfL002e1JzyEpZWkKtaXWF5FJ1jZFOjgiQKEfcbnw
Link to Amazon Page Paperback - https://www.amazon.com/RENEWAL-Heal-Heart-Your-Renewal/dp/B0GD92153W

Link to Amazon Ebook –

https://www.amazon.com/RENEWAL-Heal-Heart-Your-Renewal-ebook/
dp/B0G91BMFND

SCAN ME –

Renewal 7: Heal the Heart of Your Home in 7 Days
The Renewal Series — Family Unity Edition

Link to Paperback - https://shop.ingramspark.com/b/
084?params=nSEElv9oUsItOu5akVZlg4ycGbbmvlBOtSiqeOZr5yQ

Link to Amazon paperback - https://www.amazon.com/RENEWAL-
MARRIAGE-Heart-Marriage-Renewal/dp/B0GDC1YZJ7

Link to Amazon Ebook - https://www.amazon.com/RENEWAL-MARRIAGE-Heart-Marriage-Renewal-ebook/dp/B0G6JXJWJL

THE THRONE OF THE HEART – 12 battles we must win

AMAZON EBOOK - https://www.amazon.com/THRONE-HEART-COVETOUSNESS-Counterfeit-CONTENTMENT-ebook/dp/B0G4SPFRY7

Amazon paperback - https://www.amazon.com/THRONE-HEART-COVETOUSNESS-Counterfeit-CONTENTMENT/dp/B0G4TKW1ND

PAPERBACK FROM INGRAMSPARK - https://shop.ingramspark.com/b/084?params=a75LJXtvvI63VnzeQPleQTkAJWfu8CPQV6l5Oe31D80

4 IN 1 SERMONS BY ZACHARIAS Godseagle with Audio link –

AMAZON EBOOK LINK - https://www.amazon.com/Sermons-Zacharias-Godseagle-Audio-links-ebook/dp/B0G4XCH4TW

Amazon paperback - https://www.amazon.com/Sermons-Zacharias-Godseagle-Audio-links/dp/B0G4TK4XGT

Paperback Ingram spark link - https://shop.ingramspark.com/b/084?params=nK2JERskkbhdAOSNseTUNRhaCFqUPZuhB4uYfqrXvGb

EBOOK - https://www.amazon.com/Logos-Protocol-Awakening-artificial-intelligence-ebook/dp/B0FXNQFSWZ

Paperback - https://www.amazon.com/Logos-Protocol-Awakening-artificial-intelligence/dp/B0FXNGR66D

Hardback - https://www.amazon.com/Logos-Protocol-Awakening-artificial-intelligence/dp/B0FZNTQR6Y

Paperback Ingramspark - https://shop.ingramspark.com/b/084?params=QkK4aNYTYO9U5z9uOkdHgc7Ue1eGDLqbb1tz9WRPaSk

Why Deliverance Fails - and How the Fire of God Restores the Soul: 40 Daily Declarations for All-Round Deliverance

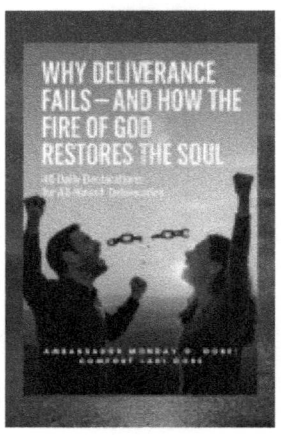

Ebook - https://www.amazon.com/Why-Deliverance-Fails-Declarations-All-Round-ebook/dp/B0FW74L4G4
Paperback - https://www.amazon.com/Why-Deliverance-Fails-Declarations-All-Round/dp/B0FWB3LXRM

Saved but Lost – The Undiscipled Convert – translated into 25 language

Paperback

https://shop.ingramspark.com/b/
084?params=iYNB6S3PLMfREpm0jMM15bMe3BvWlkjcYyLYnHVGAds

Ebook - https://www.amazon.com/SAVED-BUT-LOST-
UNDISCIPLED-heartbreak-ebook/dp/B0FVJ29DF7

7 DAYS OF SPIRITUAL WARFARE & RECOVERY - this is Part 1
Binding the Enemy, Returning Arrows Sevenfold, and Restoring Your
Destiny

https://shop.ingramspark.com/b/
084?params=8mPzqUl73Ex7uPyeO7ydyt8EGkkB6u2gX1jZvWU8j1C

E-book link - https://www.amazon.com/DAYS-SPIRITUAL-
WARFARE-RECOVERY-Returning-ebook/dp/B0FMPJM5KZ
7 DAYS OF SPIRITUAL WARFARE & RECOVERY - Part 2 - Sealing
the Victory, Breaking Household Wickedness, and Preserving Your
Restored Destiny

Paperback - https://shop.ingramspark.com/b/
084?params=LkpNmGSsApHhWhiSO7bW3wFmcXQKIO4ZEBeSbP5rL1S
Ebook - https://www.amazon.com/DAYS-SPIRITUAL-WARFARE-
RECOVERY-Wickedness-ebook/dp/B0FR9YCMY8

FROM DARKNESS TO DOMINION: 40 Days to Break Free from the Hidden Grip of Darkness

A Global Devotional of Awareness, Deliverance & Power - For Individuals, Families, and Nations Ready to Be Free

Paperback
https://shop.ingramspark.com/b/
084?params=aVgp21QfwJxNANkfMxIQ0yejuFCVY12KFr978SRkZUD
Amazon Link - https://www.amazon.com/DARKNESS-DOMINION-
Devotional-Awareness-Deliverance-ebook/dp/B0FLDH2Y67

- *Delivered from the Power of Darkness* (**Paperback**) — Buy Here[1] | Ebook on Amazon[2]

- **Top Reviews from the United States:**
  - ○ **Kindle Customer**: "The Best Christian read ever!" (5 stars)

Praise Jesus for this testimony. I have been so blessed and would recommend every one to read this book... For the wages of sin is death but the gift of God is eternal life. Shalom! Shalom!

- **Da Gster**: "This is a very interesting and rather strange book." (5 stars)

If what is said in the book is true then we really are way behind on what the enemy is capable of doing! ... A must for anyone wanting to learn about spiritual warfare.

- **Visa**: "Love this book" (5 stars)

---

1. https://shop.ingramspark.com/b/084?params=oeYbAkVTC5ao8PfdVdzwko7wi6IQimgJY2779NaqG4e

2. https://www.amazon.com/Delivered-Power-Darkness-AFRICAN-DELIVERED-ebook/dp/
   B0CC5MM4MV

This is an eye opener... a true confession... Recently I have been searching for it everywhere to buy it. So happy to get it from Amazon.

- **FrankJM**: "Quite different" (4 stars)

This book reminds me how real spiritual warfare is. It also brings to mind the reason for putting on the "Full Armor of God."

- **JenJen**: "Everyone who wants to go to Heaven- read this!" (5 stars)

This book changed my life so much. Together with John Ramirez's testimony, it will make you look at your faith differently. I've read it 6 times!

- *Ex-Satanist: The James Exchange* (Paperback) — Buy Here[3] | Ebook on Amazon[4]

---

3. https://shop.ingramspark.com/b/

084?params=I2HNGtbqJRbal8OxU3RMTApQsLLxcUCTC8zUdzDy0W1

4. https://www.amazon.com/JAMESES-Exchange-Testimony-High-Ranking-Encounters-ebook/dp/

B0DJP14JLH

- **TESTIMONY OF AN African EX-SATANIST** - *Pastor JONAS LUKUNTU MPALA* (Paperback) — Buy Here[5] | Ebook on Amazon[6]

- *Greater Exploits 14* (Paperback) — Buy Here[7] | Ebook on Amazon[8]

---

5. https://shop.ingramspark.com/b/
   084?params=0Aj9Sze4cYoLM5OqWrD20kgknXQQqO5AZYXcWtoMqWN
6. https://www.amazon.com/TESTIMONY-African-EX-SATANIST-Pastor-Jonas-ebook/dp/
   B0DJDLFKNR
7. https://shop.ingramspark.com/b/084?params=772LXinQn9nCWcgq572PDsqPjkTJmpgSqrp88b0qzKb
8. https://www.amazon.com/Greater-Exploits-MYSTERIOUS-Strategies-Countermeasures-ebook/dp/
   B0CGHYPZ8V

- *Out of the Devil's Cauldron* by John Ramirez — Available on Amazon[9]
- *He Came to Set the Captives Free* by Rebecca Brown — Find on Amazon[10]

Other books published by author – Over 1000 titles
Loved, Chosen and Whole: A 30-Day Journey from Rejection to
Restoration translated into 40 languages of the world
https://www.amazon.com/Loved-Chosen-Whole-Rejection-Restoration-ebook/dp/B0F9VSD8WL
https://shop.ingramspark.com/b/
084?params=xga0WR16muFUwCoeMUBHQ6HwYjddLGpugQHb3DVa5hE

---

9. https://www.amazon.com/Out-Devils-Cauldron-John-Ramirez/dp/0985604306

10. https://www.amazon.com/He-Came-Set-Captives-Free/dp/0883683239

In His Steps — A 40-Day WWJD Challenge:
Living Like Jesus in Real-Life Stories Around the World

https://www.amazon.com/His-Steps-Challenge-Real-Life-Stories-ebook/dp/
B0FCYTL5MG

https://shop.ingramspark.com/b/
084?params=DuNTWS59IbkvSKtGFbCbEFdv3Zg0FaITUEvlK49yLzB

JESUS AT THE DOOR:
40 Heartbreaking Stories and Heaven's Final Warning to TODAY'S Churches
https://www.amazon.com/dp/B0FDX31L9F
https://shop.ingramspark.com/b/
084?params=TpdA5j8WPvw83gIJ12N1B3nf8LQte2a1lIEy32bHcGg

COVENANT LIFE: 40 Days of Walking in the Blessing of Deuteronomy 28
- https://www.amazon.com/dp/B0FFJCLDB5
Stories from Real People, Real Obedience, and Real
https://shop.ingramspark.com/b/
084?params=bH3pzfz1zdCOLpbs7tZYJNYgGcYfU32VMz3J3a4e2Qt

Transformation in over 20 languages

KNOWING HER & KNOWING HIM:
40 Days to Healing, Understanding, and Lasting Love

https://www.amazon.com/KNOWING-HER-HIM-Healing-Understanding-ebook/dp/B0FGC4V3D9
https://shop.ingramspark.com/b/084?params=vC6KCLoI7Nnum24BVmBtSme9i6k59p3oynaZOY4B9Rd

COMPLETE, NOT COMPETE:
A 40-Day Journey to Purpose, Unity, and Collaboration

https://shop.ingramspark.com/b/
084?params=5E4v1tHgeTqOOuEtfTYUzZDzLyXLee30cqYo0Ov9941
https://www.amazon.com/COMPLETE-NOT-COMPETE-Journey-
Collaboration-ebook/dp/B0FGGL1XSQ/

DIVINE HEALTH CODE - 40 Daily Keys to Activate Healing Through
God's Word and Creation Unlock the Healing Power of Plants, Prayer, and
Prophetic Action

https://shop.ingramspark.com/b/
084?params=xkZMrYcEHnrJDhe1wuHHYixZDViiArCeJ6PbNMTbTux
https://www.amazon.com/dp/B0FHJT42TK

Other books can be found on author page https://www.amazon.com/
stores/Ambassador-Monday-O.-Ogbe/author/B07MSBPFNX